To Dad with love,
     Don, Mary + Aaron
Phil. 1:3

Dynamic Devotionals for Men

DYNAMIC DEVOTIONALS FOR MEN

WILLIAM J. KRUTZA

BAKER BOOK HOUSE
Grand Rapids, Michigan 49506

Standard Book Number: 8010-5306-4
Library of Congress Catalog Card Number: 70-138832
Copyright 1970, by Baker Book House Company
Printed in the United States of America

TO

MY SON KENNETH

who, having graduated from high school, faces the lifelong challenge of being a manly follower of Jesus Christ in today's world

MAN TO MEN

I am a man and I want to be treated like a man. When anyone approaches me with less than a straight-from-the-shoulder attitude, I'm suspicious that the challenger really is afraid that I'll tell him the truth. I don't like people who beat around the bush or tell half-truths. I always suspect there's a tinge of hyprocrisy in their way of living. They aren't really men.

When I turn to the writings of Matthew, Mark, Luke, and John, I discover that Jesus Christ was straightforward in His dealings with men. He expected men to be men. As I read of the encounters men had with Jesus Christ, at first I thought that this straightforwardness would align well with my personal straight-from-the-shoulder approach. Then I noticed how disturbing contacts with Christ can become. He never encountered a man without bringing about or demanding some kind of change in that man's life. I had to face it — He was making these demands upon my life. Thus I hope that I am writing out of my own encounters with Christ as well as about those recorded by the four gospelers.

It is not my hope that the reader will simply enjoy these pages as fillers for daily quiet times. If that is their end result, may God forever silence my typewriter. It is my hope that the reader will be disturbed and challenged as well as edified by what he reads herein. If this happens, I will consider the writing thereof a small success. If the reader is challenged to go out into our society to be a Christian man among men, my mission will have been accomplished. Hopefully each reader will have many meetings with the dynamic Christ as he meditates upon the thoughts of this little book. Then, based upon this inner reality of the living Christ, the changed man shall become a dynamic representative for the Saviour to help draw other men to the greatest life a man can live — the Christian way of life.

William J. Krutza
Wheaton, Ill.

CONTENTS

1. FIRST STEPS TO GREATNESS

Scripture: At that time the disciples came to Jesus and asked, "Who is the greatest in the kingdom of Heaven?" He called a child, set him in front of them, and said, "I tell you this: unless you turn round and become like children, you will never enter the kingdom of Heaven. Let a man humble himself till he is like this child, and he will be the greatest in the kingdom of Heaven." — *Matthew 18:1-4, New English Bible*

The church already has too many big shots; it doesn't need any more! If only men would get it into their heads that position is unimportant, the church would be a greater transforming force in the world.

Have you ever had dreams of being the greatest? Why do most of us have a passionate hope for advancement and recognition? Why do so many have the inner drive to become the head of the company? Why is there the continually recurring question, "Who shall be the greatest?" — and the jealousy when someone else is selected?

A man who seeks a position for purposes of prestige has some inner problems. Psychologists would label one of those problems "insecurity." The person has to have position to support his personality. It should be the opposite.

Having a position over others often tempts a man to think he's greater than others. He mistakenly thinks that being in authority means being better or greater than others. He forgets that at some stage of life he too was at the lower levels. He begins to rate himself: I've become important to the company. The company needs me more than it needs others.

A man can become important, especially if he gives it enough contemplation.

Throughout the centuries, men have contemplated being the

greatest. Church people have been no different. Who's greatest in the church? Is it a Billy Graham who has drawn thousands to the Saviour? Is it a Keith Miller who has challenged evangelicals through best-selling books that pierce the soul? Is it a Kenneth Taylor who has paraphrased the Scriptures into everyday language? Is it some theologian who has popularized theology? Is it some socially-minded Christian who has taken the gospel into the ghetto?

Who is your candidate? Do you have enough signatures on your petition to get his name on the ballot? How many other names will appear? Would you secretly, or not so secretly, like to sneak your own name among the candidates? Who is qualified to do the voting? Who sets the voting standards? How would candidates campaign, or would they be allowed to campaign? Would you vote for yourself? What if you only got one vote? Even if your candidate (or you) won, how would you be sure that your designation had validity or acceptance?

Here's where we come smack dab against what Jesus said about this subject. As far as He was concerned, the first step to greatness wasn't a rigged election. Even if one disciple won out in the voting, that wouldn't have been the Master's way of selecting a winner. He proposed a difficult, manly approach.

Instead of measuring the quantity of popularity to determine greatness, Christ talked about qualities that produce greatness. And what He said seemed in juxtaposition to the thinking of the disciples. He didn't even make a list of the great qualities one could expect in a great person. Rather, He simply gave a vivid, living illustration of the main quality He'd list for greatness.

A small child walked by. Jesus called the child and set him in front of them, and said, "Unless you turn round and become like children, you will never enter the kingdom of Heaven. Let a man humble himself till he is like this child, and he will be the greatest in the kingdom of Heaven."

First, Christ challenged these men to make sure they were going to get into heaven. His first comparison was: Become as a child or you'll never enter the kingdom. You need childlike dependence upon the Saviour to guarantee entrance to heaven. Arguments

12

about "who's greatest" don't reveal faith. The arrogant trust themselves. They won't make it!

Then Jesus went on to say: "Let a man humble himself till he is like this child." The humble man, one who is unpretentious as a child in his attitudes toward God, has a claim to greatness. But of course that man will never toss his hat into the "I am the greatest" ring. He'd shun any attempt by others to put him on the ballot. He'd live and die doing what he's supposed to do in the kingdom of heaven. And when he's selected — somewhere in eternity he'll still refuse to stand.

Whose ballot are you on? On the disciples' ballot or on Christ's ballot? The real man makes sure and then goes out to live accordingly!

Prayer: I confess, Lord, that I've always thought myself to be a rather great guy. Now I see that without Your grace, I'll never make it into Your kingdom. Give me the faith and open-faced attitude of a child, not only to enter Your kingdom, but to be a good representative of Yours while living in the kingdom of men. Amen.

2. MISSING THE POINT

Scripture: How is it that you do not understand that I did not speak to you about bread, when I said, keep on guarding yourself against the yeast of the Pharisees and the Sadducees? — *Matthew 16:11, Williams*

Some men get so hung up on their views of how to interpret Scripture that they not only miss the point — they actually misinterpret the text. They even become obnoxious by insisting that the Bible can only be interpreted in the manner that they have chosen. This is especially true of biblical literalists.

Rather than winning people to their viewpoint, they usually

outlast opposition to their arguments. Quite often they lose friends — especially prospective converts to Christ. But argue they will — until the hour when their throats become hoarse!

Unfortunately this stance is nothing new. The disciples were having the same problem. Jesus had warned the twelve to have nothing to do with the leaven of the Pharisees and Sadducees. Possibly P and S leaven would make them sick. What a relief when some of them reported to Jesus, "We have bought no bread."

Concern about their stomachs produced a surface, literal interpretation of the words of Christ. Jesus didn't mean it in the manner in which they meant it. What a time for Jesus to be making questioning remarks about the possibility of contaminating yeast! They were hungry.

Sure, they were well aware of the fact that leaven could spoil. But now they had an additional fear — the enemies of Jesus would try to slip in a little contaminated yeast to make the disciples sick. Maybe P and S leaven would produce death!

Jesus went along with their literalistic reasoning for a while. He reminded them of His fast-rising, fully-baked dough at the feeding of the five thousand and at the feeding of the four thousand. If they had to be literalists, let them recall His involvement in making gigantic quantities of eatable bread.

Then He abruptly stopped them in their approach. "How is it that you do not understand that I did not speak to you about bread?" How could they be so dense? Couldn't they understand that the leavening agent of these religious sects had nothing to do with bread? How could they fail to recognize that the Pharisees and Sadducees had no intentions of peddling bakery ingredients?

But that's the trouble when a person insists on always being a biblical literalist. Such a person will never consider the possibility or plausibility of the figurative interpretation. Consequently, he, like the disciples, is in danger of missing the true meaning of the Word of God.

The disciples, like thousands since, were really puzzled by another statement of the Saviour. In presenting the meaning of

14

His death, He proclaimed that unless they ate His flesh and drank His blood they could not partake of His ministry to them. Surely He didn't mean it literally! If He did, how could they fulfill His statement?

The church has had some real problems with this text. The literalists — in the present case the Roman Catholics — have insisted on their own "true" church. Protestants, most of whom take a figurative approach to this statement, have also gone their own ways. Interestingly enough, Bible-pounding literalists take this passage figuratively. How's come?

Whenever a man insists that he has an ironclad approach to the Word of God, he's apt to miss some of the true meaning of that Word. Being open to the most plausible interpretation will bring great benefit. Being open to the meaning that the manly Christ wants to impart is most rewarding. It can also be dangerous and demanding.

Looking straight into their eyes, He challenged the disciples' simplistic views. Fortunately they understood their error; they understood that He was warning them against the distorted doctrines of the Pharisees and Sadducees.

A mature man doesn't clamor for a simplistic interpretation of the words of Christ. The manly fellow isn't afraid to go deeper to get the meaning the Lord really intended.

How often does your approach to the Bible interfere with what God actually wants to say to you? How often do your pre-interpretations actually keep the Spirit from breaking into your experience? How often does Christ have to say to you, "How is it that you do not understand?" How often do you really miss the point even though you pride yourself in having the right interpretation?

But there is hope for those who'll be men — "then they understood."

Prayer: Lord, though I've developed quite a foolproof approach to Your Word, don't let this interfere with the actual meanings that You want to communicate to me. Penetrate my mind, by

Your Spirit, with all the possibilities that can be developed. Then give me the wisdom to select the most biblical approach. Amen.

3. WHAT ARE THE MEN OF THIS GENERATION LIKE?

Scripture: And the Lord said, To what, then, shall I compare the men of this generation? What are they like? They put me in mind of those children who call to their companions as they sit in the marketplace and say, You would not dance when we piped to you, you would not mourn when we wept to you. — *Luke 7:31, 32, Knox*

Was Jesus guilty of making a gross generalization? How could He put all men of "this generation" into one category? If He were around today, would He have been able to make the same type of statement? Could what He said be applied to all men at all times in history? If so, why is what He said so universally true?

Answering Christ's questions in twentieth-century lingo might prove quite interesting. Or on second thought, first or even twenty-first-century terminology might fit. To what can Christ compare our generation? What are today's men really like?

Let's first separate the men from the boys. Boys, up until they have home responsibilities, usually haven't settled into any ruts. They're usually adventurous enough to respond to the piping they hear. In fact, too often they jump from one idea to another depending upon the tone of the call or the person of the caller.

But men like to think of themselves as mature. By this they mean a certain amount of stability in employment, in marriage, in philosophy of life, in acceptance of church doctrines, in political principles. Rarely will a man admit to much immaturity — that's the main characteristic of boys. And when I became a man, Paul said, I gave up childish things.

16

One must constantly be on guard that his thought of maturity isn't simply a cover up for a lack of ambition or a fear of change. A mature person has the ability to hear the "piping" of the age in which he lives and to make appropriate changes in his manner of thinking and living. A mature person is sensitive to the "piping" of those around him, constantly aware of their desires and their outlook on life.

What Jesus said about the generation of men to whom He was speaking was that they were insensitive to what was happening around them. As Williams translates this section, "We played the wedding march to you, but you did not dance; we sang the funeral dirge, and you did not mourn." The men were totally unaffected by either joy or sorrow. They weren't inspired to tap their toes when the wedding party arrived with music and dancing. Nor did they possess any sorrowing emotions. They couldn't shed a tear at a funeral. Hardness of heart destroyed their ability to express their emotions. It also destroyed their ability to make correct judgments. This is brought out clearly in the next verses where they make accusations against both Christ and John the Baptist.

But have we become so apathetic that we can't get joyously excited with those who rejoice or sincerely sorrowful with those who mourn? Have we become so calloused to what happens around us — especially calamity — that we fail to recognize what produces joy? Have we heard the wedding march and simply gazed at the marchers without smiling? Have we heard the funeral song and not become emotionally involved with those who have lost a loved one?

For some men the greatest achievement is to maintain the status quo. They don't want to be disturbed, so they carefully build protections around their emotions. If they ever laugh it has to be limited. They never cry — it's unmanly.

How easy to fall into this attitude. How easy to equate spiritual maturity with an ability to control emotions. How easy to think we've arrived when we can remain poker-faced regardless of the occasion. How easy to even begin to believe that mirth is sinful or that it shows spiritual weakness when a man cries.

To what could Christ compare an emotionless man? Would He find as many in today's computerized world as He did then? Probably He'd find more — many whose lives are as programmed as any computer system. There's not much to which anyone could compare an emotionless man. That's why Christ had difficulty finding an appropriate simile.

He's still looking for those whose emotions and judgments inspire response. He likes to see even real he-men laugh and cry. That's what makes a man a real man. How much better for Him to compare us to an excited wedding party or a group of sorrowful mourners. With such emotions we won't usually make too many incorrect, hardhearted responses. We'll give evidence that even our emotions have been brought into harmony with our Lord.

Prayer: Jesus, give me the ability to laugh and to cry. Couple with this the sensitivity I need to know at which time I should do which one. Amen.

4. WHERE WOULD YOU LIKE TO SIT IN HEAVEN?

Scripture: James and John, the sons of Zebedee, approached him and said, "Master, we should like you to do us a favour." "What is it you want me to do?" he asked. They answered, "Grant us the right to sit in state with you, one at your right and the other at your left." Jesus said to them, "You do not understand what you are asking." — *Mark 10:35-38, New English Bible*

The audacity of those two fellows — to ask that they have the most stately positions in the kingdom of Christ. Who did they think they were?

We might let them off the hook a little if we took Matthew's account of the incident. Matthew says that their mother made

18

the request. But when Christ's answer is considered (even that recorded by Matthew), they were right back on the hook. He answered the two *men*.

After being such a long time under the teaching of the Master, it's quite odd that they make such a request. Hadn't He recently given them His description of greatness by placing a child among them? Hadn't He been able to communicate to them that those who humbled themselves and became servants were eligible for the best rewards? Hadn't they caught the vision of forgetting self in ministry to others?

If we interpreted this from a "sitting at the feet of Jesus" stance, then the logic of wanting to continue that position eternally could be justified. But the text doesn't warrant such an approach. They didn't make their request out of humility or out of the desire to learn. They made it out of a desire to have positions of importance. To sit nearest to a royal person, whether to the right or to the left of that person, meant to have a favored position. Such a position combined authority with prestige. That's what James and John had in mind.

But have you ever honestly asked yourself, "Where would I like to sit in heaven?" No glib answer will suffice. Nor will what you've piously stated in some Sunday school class. Deep down in your personality, what answer would you give? Would you really want an unnoticed position or is your name James or John?

Some men, because they have had little recognition upon earth or few prestigious jobs in the church, secretly desire a place of position in heaven. They'd like to sit to the left or the right of Christ to make up for getting kicked around during this life. Secretly they think God owes them something for what they've done for Him. Though they'd never admit this secret ambition, the Lord says to their innermost being, "You do not understand what you are asking."

Some men think they'll naturally "sit in state" with Jesus because they've had positions of importance and recognition while upon earth. Unless their personalities are drastically changed in that split second in which they enter the presence of Christ, they'll be disappointed if they don't get the desired position. They've never considered that Jesus said, "The first shall be last," as well as, "The last shall be first."

The two disciples didn't get much satisfaction out of Christ's answers to where they'd like to sit in heaven. "It's not for you or Me to know or decide" was the essence of His reply. Besides, let's let heaven's matters take care of themselves. Right now there's something far more important for you fellows to consider: "Can you suffer with Me?"

They said they could. He said they would. And the reward was up to the Father.

Where do you want to sit in heaven? Suffer with Him, share in the ministry of His cross, be willing to give your whole life to His kingdom's causes — and you'll be so involved with Him you'll forget all about the superfluous, unanswerable questions.

But if you're not manly enough for that, keep asking. There's always another disciple who's willing to waste his time arguing with you about the position of the chairs in heaven.

Prayer: Lord, because of my egocentricities, I've often become overly concerned about what's going to happen to me in the hereafter. Draw me away from position-seeking so I'll more fully accomplish Your program in the world and radiate more of Your personal characteristics as You live in me. After all, since I'll see and enjoy You forever, what difference does it make if I'm first in line? Amen.

5. WHAT KIND OF CHRIST DO YOU HAVE?

Scripture: So he took a ship, and his disciples followed him. And suddenly a great storm arose on the sea, so that the waves rose high over the ship; but he lay asleep. And his disciples came and roused him, crying, Lord, save us, we are sinking. Jesus said to them, Why are you faint-hearted, men of little faith? Then he rose up, and checked the winds, and the sea, and there was deep calm. So that all asked in amazement, What kind of man is this, who is obeyed even by the winds and the sea? — *Matthew 8:23-27, Knox*

The disciples' Christ got tired and needed to sleep; our Christ doesn't. The disciples' Christ needed a conveyance in order to travel across a little Palestinian lake; our Christ doesn't. Our Christ, who rose from the dead and ascended into heaven to sit at the right hand of the Father, no longer limits Himself by physical factors.

This should make all the difference in the world as far as our concepts of His authority and power are concerned. But does it? What would we call Him to do in the crises of our lives? What do we expect Him to do for us here and now — when there is no crisis? How much faith do we have that He'll hear and answer us and show us what Jeremiah talked about — "great and mighty things which we know not at present"?

If you've ever been fishing in a small boat on a rough lake, you can sense something of the anxiety of the disciples. Waves splash against the boat. Water gets inside. You struggle to get back to your point of departure or else to the other shore. You even have thoughts of what it's like to live like a fish. What would you do if the boat overturned? The disciples — several of whom had had long experience with Galilean waves — became desperate and frightened. They were sinking. And like Jonah of Old Testament fame, you guessed it, Jesus was sleeping comfortably.

Notice, it was in desperation, not in faith, that the disciples roused Jesus and shouted into His ears, "Lord, save us, we are sinking." Jesus' answer indicated that their motivation wasn't one of faith. He asked them, "Why are you faint-hearted, men of little faith?"

If they had believed in Christ's power, they would have approached Him differently or else He would have responded differently. He responded in answer to their inner attitudes.

It might be good, then, to stop right here and ask yourself: Do I really believe in Christ to the extent that I'm sure He'd change my circumstances almost immediately if I cried unto Him? In my times of need, do I cry out more in desperation because I can't do anything more to change the situation, or do I cry out because of an abiding confidence in the authority and power of Christ?

Knowing that the disciples were completely helpless in the situation, Jesus stood up and told the winds and the waves to be calm. They obeyed, of course!

At that point, the disciples asked the question among themselves, "What kind of man is this, who is obeyed even by the winds and the sea?" They still weren't quite sure how to take this Christ. What kind of a man was He? Was He everything He claimed to be? Was He much more than a man? Was He some kind of a god? Was He God?

It's in some of the crisis hours that we really find out how great Christ really is. Christ proves Himself most powerful, most interested in our problems. Even the natural laws seem to be overruled by His ways and words. He performs His acts — miracles! He heals. He gives special insight into problems. He opens new opportunities to us.

At crisis hours we also find out what motivates us to call upon Christ for assistance. For the man who has had a constant and continuous reliance upon the Lord, his inner faith turns him naturally in Christ's direction. To whom else would the faith-filled man go? It's as normal to turn to the Lord in times of need as it is to turn to a water faucet in times of thirst.

But for the man who has been considerably self-reliant — like many of us tend to be about much of life — turning to Christ is more of a last-ditch effort. Such a man tries everything else first. He tries to bail out the water. He tries to row harder. He appeals to others around him to lend a helping hand. Finally when nothing else can help, when he's entirely out of strength and resources, he thinks about God.

Unfortunately, too many of us who say we really trust Christ take this approach. We think it's more manly. But the truly manly fellow knows his limitations even before the crisis comes. He also knows the limitlessness of the Lord — and places complete confidence in Him.

What kind of Christ do you have? It all depends on what you think of yourself! It all depends on whether you're man enough to recognize Him for what He really is!

Prayer: Lord, I've proclaimed, "You are the Christ, the Son of God." I've called You my Saviour. Yet so often I still find myself trusting myself, as if You didn't matter in my life. Supply the humility and faith to reverse the situation so my saying You are Lord will really express the way I live as well as the way I speak. Amen.

6. WHEN THE WORD IS AIMED AT YOU

Scripture: The lawyers and chief priests wanted to lay hands on him there and then, for they saw that this parable was aimed at them; but they were afraid of the people. — *Luke 20:19, New English Bible*

Jesus had what many present-day church parishioners might label a bad habit when practiced by a local pastor. The Master aimed His messages at His hearers. He didn't talk to people who weren't all present and accounted for. He didn't direct the pungent preachments at faraway governmental leaders. He didn't preach about the terrible sinners who never came within earshot of His evangelistic outbursts. He didn't expound about people or theories related to a nation that existed two thousand years previously.

The Master Preacher spoke to His audience. He fit His sermons to the occasion. Situation preaching, you'd have to call it. As far as He was concerned, the people who needed a word from Him on any given occasion were those who saw His lips move, who heard the inflections of His voice, who noticed how He gestured toward them.

It's that kind of preaching that gets the preacher into difficulty with his listeners. Somehow that kind of preaching always pricks hearers' hearts. Somehow the preacher is always burning someone's ears. Somehow the words from such a preacher's lips penetrate the personalities of the hearers. Somehow such sermons disturb the status quo. Somehow such a preacher often incites violent responses.

But if a preacher today is to follow the preaching pattern of the Master, then he'd better prepare to receive the type of responses the Master received. He'd better have a thick skin. He'd better learn not to get hurt feelings. He'd better maintain a friend-to-Friend basis with the Master from whom he can draw strength and encouragement.

Thank God there are such preachers around, although they are few in number. Too many preachers (even those who are old-fashioned Bible thumpers) have succumbed to the demands of their hearers. They have found the formula that fits what hearers want to hear — anything that lambasts nonpresent sinners, that talks about the corruption in society, that expounds particular Bible texts with little or no present-day application. Thank God if your pastor disturbs you when you listen to his sermons. Thank God if he forces you to reexamine your faith. Thank God if he demands that you take your Christianity into the marketplace. Thank God if he challenges you to change your course of concern to include those who suffer injustices in our society. Thank God — and then react in a soul-searching, life-involving manner.

Unfortunately, we don't read that the religious leaders, the fundamentalists of Christ's day, reacted in this manner. They did what some congregations have done when a pastor preaches too much of an up-to-date gospel — they sought to get rid of Him. If only they could have called their congregation together and democratically followed a synagogue constitution: A preacher can only be removed if a petition containing X number of signatures and a two-thirds majority supports the petition in a special meeting. But, fortunately for us and for the world, the itinerant Jesus couldn't be treated in that twentieth-century manner.

Because they didn't want to follow the teachings of Jesus Christ, every chance they had they sought to get rid of Him. Eventually they succeeded — not to His defeat, but to theirs! How much better would the story have turned out if they had admitted they were in a wrong relationship to Him and to God? How much better if they would have confessed their hardness of heart and surrendered to His leadership?

But can we stand in judgment of these men? Do we not need to look into our own hearts and ask ourselves: How do I react when the Word is aimed at me? How do I respond when the preacher's words sock it to me? Do I build a resentment against God's spokesman or do I respond in a positive manner?

Paul said that some men have the special gift of prophecy — of forthtelling as well as foretelling — for the edification of the believers. We'd better believe him. And if we do, we're going to find our local pastor socking it to us, telling it like it is, and then we'll do something about his messages.

It's up to you how you react. The way you do will tell whether you, like those to whom Jesus was speaking, want to lay hands on God's messenger or volunteer to do something about what he declares. The way you react will either retard or advance the kingdom in your life, community, and world.

Prayer: Lord, I admit I've often reacted against Your preachers because they've periodically stepped on my toes. Forgive me. Help me to draw from every sermon those challenges that would order my life more in line with Your will. Thank You for every straightforward challenge that shall come my way. Amen.

7. REPUTATION OR CHARACTER

Scripture: There were, for all that, many of the rulers who had learned to believe in him; but they would not profess it because of the Pharisees, afraid of being forbidden the synagogue. They valued their credit with men higher than their credit with God. — *John 12:42, 43, Knox*

Secret believers — that's the name we give to those who say they believe on Christ and yet haven't the courage to stand out for Him. Secret believers — that's the name we give to those who are believers in communist-dominated countries, who, if they stood out for Christ, would be severely restricted or martyred.

But the secret believers among the elite "rulers who had learned to believe in him" weren't simply hiding for fear of death. It was more a fear of losing prestige and position. They cherished the important positions in the synagogue. They reveled in the acclaim of the people. They enjoyed looking around as they entered the synagogue. They wanted to see that they were recognized. It was good to hear others say, "Glad to see you in the synagogue this morning."

To identify with Christ almost assured them that their pomp and recognition would be terminated. In fact, they'd be numbered among the group of Christ's followers — the group that the Pharisees detested. They'd be blackballed from this snobbish religious fraternity. Who was willing to give up such an illustrious heritage simply to follow a lowly, tax collector-loving Galilean?

They believed they could enjoy the best of both lives. They could be secret believers. Among those of like faith they could share the secret of their personal belief in Jesus Christ. They could even enjoy a limited amount of fellowship in His name. But they better be careful. They couldn't afford the presence of a Pharisee. He just might tell everyone else their secrets.

How quickly people, even twentieth-century Christian men,

can get their sense of values inverted. Of these rulers, John writes, "They valued their credit with men higher than their credit with God." Simple as that, their reputations were more important than their characters.

Before we condemn them, let's look at ourselves. Have there ever been occasions when we backed off from a clear-cut identification with Jesus Christ? When an identification with Him in some social setting would have produced some jeers or ridicule, did we back down and simply not say anything that would indicate our allegiance to Christ? When others were boasting of their lack of faith, or their trust in their own wisdom or money, did you boldly talk about your faith in God? Have you ever been silent when you should have shouted?

Really, one of the underlying reasons for their valuing their credit with men higher than their credit with God was simply their misconception of God. Their God was too small. Their reputations among men were their actual gods. The living, all powerful deity really hadn't been grasped in full measure by their minds. They were afraid of men when they should have been fearing God. They were more concerned about what temporal people would say than about what an eternal God could say. They based their lives upon human praise rather than upon divine principles.

What form this takes in your life only you can know. What do you really think about Jesus Christ? Is He simply some far-off Saviour who holds the policy and pays the premium on your eternal assurance? Is He someone upon whom you draw for wisdom, power, and other Christian virtues only when you think these will benefit you? Or is He all that He proclaimed Himself to be — especially as He relates to your life as Lord?

When a man values his standing with God, he isn't too fearful about the reputation he has among snobbish men. Surely he wants to be a useful servant among men, but his eyes are on a higher goal — pleasing his Lord. He wants to influence men Godward and not turn them away because of some kink in his personality, but he wants to represent Jesus Christ boldly and honorably. He wants the credit sheet to be in the black on God's side regardless of whether men use red ink when speaking about him. Character, controlled by the Holy Spirit, is far superior to reputation conceived by men.

Prayer: Holy Spirit, give me the courage to identify myself unreservedly with Jesus Christ not only among those who believe like I do, but among those who scoff at the idea of surrendering to Him. Help me to put the integrity of true character before any idea of reputation regardless of how much praise could easily come my way. In the name of the honest Christ. Amen.

8. JOINING CHRIST'S FISHING CREW

Scripture: As He was walking by the shore of the sea of Galilee, He saw two brothers, Simon who was surnamed Peter, and his brother, Andrew, casting a net into the sea, for they were fishermen. He said to them, "Come! Follow me, and I will make you fishermen for catching men." — *Matthew 4:18-20, Williams*

Jesus never took a Dale Carnegie course. Yet He continually demonstrated the principles of winning people to Himself and influencing them to change their ways of living. Walking along the shore of Palestine's best fishing lake, He spotted two fishermen. He decided they'd make good "catchers of men."

Since fishermen usually have considerable time to gawk at what's going on on shore, these two brothers probably recognized Jesus. "See that fellow. Isn't He the prophet who has been stirring things up around Galilee? What do you think He's up to now?"

Just about that time, they saw Jesus stop at the edge of the lake, beckon toward them in their boat, and shout out to them, "Follow me, and I will make you fishermen for catching men."

Typical of His method of approach, Jesus used the known to lead these fellows into the unknown. No theological jargon for

28

these boys. They wouldn't have understood. They were accustomed to seaside slang. They perked up when someone talked about fish, nets, boats, fishermen's luck.

Why church workers haven't learned the simplicity of the Master's approach is difficult to understand. Too many present-day Christians are so wrapped up in their evangelical terminology that they don't even care if the hearers understand. In fact, some suspect anyone who doesn't mouth the right cliches.

To these types of people, witnessing seems to be more an obligation to be fulfilled than a compassionate approach to win a hearing. Jesus immediately won a hearing — and two fishy-smelling disciples!

Even though Jesus used language they'd understand, He used it to further His purpose. Taking the known, He called them into the unknown. Through a direct challenge to their present understanding, He demanded a commitment to what they did not understand. He didn't tell them to think it through. He didn't explain how a fish fisherman could become a catcher of men. He didn't say they could be both at the same time.

It was the Master's manly approach that appealed to these net casters. It's the approach you can expect from the manly Christ — if you're a real man. No beating around the bush. No half-way discipleship. No call to be less than you are at the present. But a demand to make a clear-cut decision. A demand to a more challenging type of life. A demand that you turn your back on your present way of life if it doesn't fit in with His plans. A demand that you fully follow Him.

How will you respond? "Sure, Jesus, I'll follow You, but let me take along my own tackle box. . . . I'll follow You, but let me fish only where I think they'll 'bite' the gospel. . . . I'll follow You, on a part-time basis. You know, Jesus, I still have my own boat anchored by my lakeside cabin!"

Happily, the history of the New Testament church reveals that these two robust fishermen didn't respond in any of these modern men's ways. Their responses were in perfect harmony with the invitation of the manly Christ. He said, "Come!" They came. He said, "Follow me." Immediately they dropped their nets and followed Him. He said, "I will make you fishermen for catching men." And the New Testament gives several instances in which these two fishermen netted people into the kingdom. On one occasion, people-fishing Peter had a catch of three thousand souls.

Whether you've had your first or one hundred and first encounter with the manly Christ, don't expect anything less than a demanding challenge to forsake your attachment to your present way of life when He says, "Follow Me." For an exciting, adventurous, and possibly dangerous way of life, trust your life into His hands. He's looking for real manly fellows to join His fishing crew.

Prayer: Lord, thanks for making a man-sized demand upon my life. I'm tired of hearing about "take it or leave it" types of Christianity. I understand Your call and am willing to follow You regardless of the consequences. Transform my talents and interests into useful means for the development of Your kingdom. Amen.

9. NO MORE NIGHTTIME DISCIPLESHIP

Scripture: Then one of their number, Nicodemus (the man who had once visited Jesus), intervened. "Does our law," he asked them, "permit us to pass judgement on a man unless we have first given him a hearing and learned the facts?" "Are you a Galilean too?" they retorted. "Study the scriptures and you will find that prophets do not come from Galilee." — *John 7:50-52, New English Bible*

We're all familiar with John 3, the account of Nicodemus coming to Jesus by night. We've probably accepted the commonly proposed reasons why he chose the after-dark hour: he feared that the other Jewish leaders would catch him speaking to Christ; he didn't want others to think that he was identifying with the Messiah.

That nighttime encounter produced one of the basic concepts of evangelical Christianity: Ye must be born again. Men throughout the centuries have appealed to this passage in directing people Christward. Today, verses from John 3 are some of the first words of Scripture memorized by Sunday school pupils. And if you sought the central theme verse to express the gospel, you'd probably quote John 3:16.

But Nicodemus wasn't concerned about all the theology that would develop out of his nighttime encounter with deity. He was simply interested in learning, in a personal way, something about the majestic teaching ability of the One people were calling Messiah, Master, Son of God. There was no substitute for a face-to-face encounter. So Nicodemus came to Jesus for a nighttime appointment.

Instead of being so negative, let's give Nicodemus credit for his evening venture. Possibly our interpretation of why he came after dark shouldn't impugn his character as strongly as has been done. Possibly his daily duties kept him busy so personal interests had to wait until the afterwork hours. Maybe the nighttime appointment was the first convenient private time in the schedule of the busy Christ.

The significance of the encounter is that he did come to Jesus, not what time the clock might have said. When he got there, the directness of his good questioning showed his deep interest in learning the Master's approach to life. He asked soul-searching questions and Jesus came up with dynamic answers. And though Nicodemus had difficulty in his literalistic approach to the words of Christ, still he was left with making a choice. The only missing ingredient in the John 3 text seems to be what every fundamentalist desires when the gospel is presented the first time to a sinner — an immediate decision to sign up with Christ.

By the time we get to John 7, we notice that a change has taken place in Nicodemus. He doesn't appear to be the questioning ruler of the Jews. Rather, he is defending the right of Christ to be heard before others condemn Him. He was speaking out of experience. He had gotten the facts from Jesus; he had given Christ a hearing before he made a judgment. This was in harmony with Jewish law and tradition.

This defense of Jesus automatically brought Nicodemus out of the dark. And his future identification with Jesus did the same. There came a time in his life when he could no longer be a nighttime disciple. If he wouldn't make a personal identification, others would do it for him. Thus he had to come out of the dark.

Possibly you are a nighttime disciple. You have encountered the teachings of Christ in your home via discussions with your wife. Or you've attended church worship services to please her. Or you've even gone so far as to read the New Testament to find out who Christ really was. Through all this you've made up your mind — Christ is really the Saviour, the only one to whom you can commit the eternal welfare of your life. Yet you haven't told anyone of your acceptance of these facts. Even your wife, with whom you share your thinking about most of what goes on in your life, doesn't know if you're a believer.

Then suddenly you're challenged about your beliefs by some nonbeliever. He suspects that you have begun to believe the Bible. He suspects that you think that Jesus is more than a great teacher of the past. He presents the "What think you of Jesus Christ?" type of questions. Suddenly, in order to keep your integrity, you are faced with abandoning your nighttime discipleship. It's the hour about which Paul talked in Romans 10:9, "If on your lips is the confession, 'Jesus is Lord,' and in your heart the faith that God raised him from the dead, then you will find salvation" (NEB). A glorious dawning has come to your life. The Light of the World has bombarded your inner nature. You suddenly sense the meaning of the passage of the Bible that says they that walk in darkness have seen a great light. You are born again.

Nighttime discipleship will never satisfy a man who has a dynamic encounter with Light!

Prayer: Out of darkness into Your marvelous light, Jesus, I come.

Thank You for all the experiences that have led me into daytime discipleship. Help me to be a means of leading other nighttime followers of Yours out of the dark into the day. Amen.

10. DO YOU LIKE JESUS' FRIENDS?

Scripture: When Jesus was at table in the house, many bad characters — tax-gatherers and others — were seated with him and his disciples. The Pharisees noticed this, and said to his disciples, "Why is it that your master eats with tax-gatherers and sinners?" Jesus heard them and said, "It is not the healthy that need a doctor, but the sick. Go and learn what the text means 'I require mercy, not sacrifice.' I did not come to invite virtuous people, but sinners." — *Matthew 9:10-13, New English Bible*

Let another man take a good look at your friends and he'll be able to tell a lot about your character. If you're a middle-class American, you'll have middle-class friends. If you're on the social register, your friends probably will be listed there too. If you're a poor man, your friends probably struggle as much as you do to make ends meet. Most often, a person's friends are numbered among his kind.

Friends can be classified economically, politically, religiously, by sport interest, by hobbies, by job interest, and in many other ways. Interestingly enough, usually the economic factor crosses classification lines. Sometimes the other classifications are simply interest groups within the economic listing.

Then in walks the Person we call the Friend of Sinners! Wow! Our classifications suddenly get all goofed. He doesn't care whether we are rich or poor; He has a few millionaires among His followers; He has thousands of poor people. Some of His friends wear mink coats and drive new Cadillacs; others have mended hand-me-down, out-of-style jackets and come to church in old, battered compact cars. He doesn't check the automobile titles or clothing labels before He says, "Come unto me." In fact, He already said, "I am now standing at the door and knocking. If anyone listens to my voice and opens the door, I will be his guest and feast with him, and he with me" (Revelation 3:20, Williams). The only criteria: you open the door; you let Him in; He's glad to be the guest of any man.

During His stay on earth He became Friend to bad characters even more than to the good. The bad ones knew they needed His friendship; the good men were too sophisticated, too self-sufficient. Numbered among His friends: a blind beggar, a scheming tax-collector, a prostitute, an outcast leper. He became Friend to anyone who accepted His loving help. He didn't categorize people by status, by racial identity, or even on the basis that they'd become His followers. He had only one category — anyone who fit himself into that category became a friend of the Master. That divine category: those in need who wanted help.

The sophisticated, self-righteous Pharisees had their own category. And they couldn't understand how Jesus, who was a teacher, so diametrically opposed their categorization. Thus it was, that on this encounter with the disciples, the Pharisees asked, "Why does your master eat with such notorious people?"

Maybe the disciples couldn't really answer. Sometimes they even wondered why Jesus chose such hippieish-looking friends. Why did He have to bother with people who, for the most part, could do little to enhance His reputation? Luckily, Jesus heard the Pharisees. He had the perfect answer, "It is not the healthy that need a doctor, but the sick."

Any man who doesn't recognize the sickness in his soul will be bothered by the presence of Jesus. Why have this Soul Physician around if you're convinced you have a healthy inner being? He might even embarrass you if some of His real friends show up!

Jesus operates the same today as He did in Palestine. His only real friends are people who recognize themselves as needy sinners. His invitation is to whoever wants to come to Him. And make no mistake about it, more out-and-out and down-and-out sinners recognize their need of Him than the sophisticated we-make-it-on-our-own types. When he said, "I did not come to invite virtuous people, but sinners," He knew who'd accept Him.

You might as well make up your mind, if you're going to be a true friend of Jesus, and if you're going to be a friend of the friends of Jesus, you're going to have to accept people on far different criteria than those commonly proposed in our society. Maybe you'll have to bear the thought of being suspected or even rejected. But wouldn't you rather have Christ's smile upon your choice of friends? Besides, it's the people Jesus calls His friends that you'll have to live with in heaven for eternity! So you'd better come up with a good answer to the question: Do I like Jesus' friends? The answer centers in how much you really like Him!

Prayer: Man looks on the outward appearance, but You look on the heart. Correct the sight of my soul so I'll judge people by the divine standards and thus fully follow You. May more of Your friends know my address. Amen.

11. SIR, WE WANT TO SEE JESUS

Scripture: There were some Greeks among those who were coming up to worship at the feast, and they went to Philip who was from Bethsaida in Galilee, and kept making this request of him, "Sir, we want to see Jesus!" — *John 12:20, 21, Williams*

If someone walked up to you demanding that you lead them into a life-changing encounter with Jesus Christ, how would you react? Would you quote some verses from your "four things you ought to know" pamphlet? Would you take them through three, four or five spiritual laws? Would you falter for words, not knowing which Scripture texts to quote or what really to say? Would you have a formula approach?

Or would your first reactions be somewhat like Philip's (as

described by Williams)? It seems that Philip really wasn't interested in directing these Greeks to the Lord Jesus. He was either preoccupied with his own thinking and the salvation of his own soul or some other subject. His initial response seems to have been a blank stare. The Greeks had to keep on asking him, "Sir, we want to see Jesus."

This initial response of Philip is rather suggestive. He was supposedly committed to bringing people to the Saviour. Wasn't that what Christ wanted him to do as a "fisher of men"? But they had to be of his own kind. They had to fit the pattern he had envisioned. These Greeks just didn't fit the image Philip had of people who could become followers of Jesus. Surely these particular Greeks were beyond conversion. What could Christ do for them? So when they approached him with their request, the words of their cry didn't penetrate.

How readily have we developed our stereotypes of people who'll respond to the gospel? Have we put anyone beyond the reach of God's mercy because he has a different skin color? because he has had a different religious upbringing? because he hasn't stepped out of his morality system into ours? because he hasn't voiced our formula for salvation?

For quite some time Philip couldn't get beyond his stereotyped thinking. And as long as his mind and soul remained closed, the call of the needy didn't penetrate. He heard the Greeks talking but didn't fathom the depth of their cry.

Secondly, notice that even when he did hear their cry, he didn't bring the Greeks directly to Jesus. We're not quite sure why, but he went to one of the other disciples, Andrew. We might be able to understand how two would probably have a better approach than one, but what was the flimsy reason? Why direct a seeker to some person other than Christ? Why not accept the challenge of leading the seekers to the Saviour? Why not receive the Lord's personal commendation for directing them to Him? Philip missed out on these; Andrew didn't.

Andrew was more discerning. It didn't take him long to ascertain the Greeks' wishes and how they could be satisfied. To

Andrew there weren't any complicated four steps; there weren't any theological hurdles to get over or around. It was simple: bring them to Jesus; let the Master solve their search. So we read, "Andrew [notice that he's mentioned first] and Philip both went and told Jesus."

Probably Philip felt somewhat ashamed at his personal reluctance to bring the Greeks directly to Jesus; we will never know. But he surely saw how Jesus answered the inner needs of the Greeks in much the same manner He had answered Philip's personal need. Surely he also realized that the kingdom of Christ isn't limited by one disciple's concepts of who shall enter and who shall not enter. The words that John penned in the third chapter, and which Philip probably heard many times from the Saviour's lips, "that whosoever believeth in Him," took on specific meaning. The "whosoever" included these Greeks.

How much these two verses say to us. How open we ought to be to recognize seekers after God. How willing we ought to be to bring them to direct contact with Christ. How discerning we ought to be so we don't put in some intermediary steps on their heavenward way. How joyous we ought to be when the seekers find satisfaction and salvation in Jesus Christ.

If you are a Philip, for the sake of the kingdom of God it would be good if you'd change your name to Andrew!

Prayer: Spirit of God, give me a discerning heart that can detect when others are longing to meet the Saviour. Give me the patience, humility, and wisdom needed to bring them directly to Him. Let me not hinder them by demanding conformity to my stereotyped approach to You. In fact, break me out of these spiritually deadening stereotypes. Let the approach be as fresh as each person's personality. In the name of the unique Son of God. Amen.

12. CHRIST'S ANTIPOVERTY PROGRAM

Scripture: And now a man came up and asked him, "Master, what good must I do to gain eternal life?" ". . . if you wish to enter into life, keep the commandments." . . . "I have kept all these. Where do I still fall short?" Jesus said to him, "If you wish to go the whole way, go, sell your possessions, and give to the poor, and then you will have riches in heaven; and come, follow me." When the young man heard this, he went away with a heavy heart; for he was a man of great wealth. — *Matthew 19:16, 17, 20-22, New English Bible*

So you thought that the antipoverty program was some political invention of the 1960s. You didn't realize that antipoverty was instituted by God. Why all the opposition to it? Why not go beyond what the government proposes?

The wealthy fellow that came to Jesus didn't expect what he heard. He probably thought Jesus would pat him on the back and send him on his way with a challenge to keep up the good work.

Most of us would strut a little if we could pass the religious scrutiny of Jesus. This fellow claimed the ability to react both negatively and positively to the commandments at exactly the right times. He was a fundamentalist in relation to the law. He could put an "X" in the No boxes after "Have you every committed murder, adultery, theft, false witness?" His "X" also went in the Yes boxes after "honor father and mother, love neighbor as thyself." Except for the last one, which seems to be a forgotten practice in many churches that loudly proclaim that they believe the Bible, probably all of us could "X" the correct boxes. Didn't Jesus know that it is difficult to love one's neighbor as much as he loves himself?

Down deep, this fellow knew there was a missing ingredient in

38

his life. "Where do I still fall short?" he asked. It was then that Jesus proposed the divine antipoverty bit.

Hadn't the man read the Old Testament? "If there be among you a poor man . . . thou shalt not harden thine heart, nor shut thine hand from thy poor brother: But thou shalt open thine hand wide unto him, and shalt surely lend him sufficient for his need, in that he wanteth. Beware that . . . thine eye be [not] evil against thy poor brother, and thou givest him nought; and he cry unto the Lord against thee, and it be sin unto thee. . . . For the poor shall never cease out of the land: therefore I command thee, saying, Thou shalt open thy hand wide unto thy brother, to thy poor, and to thy needy, in the land" (Deuteronomy 15:7-11, KJV).

Jesus appealed to the man in this fellow — and found him still to be a selfish boy! He said to him, "If you wish to go the whole way, go, sell your possessions, and give to the poor . . . and come, follow me." Join the divine antipoverty program, Jesus told the man. Antipoverty is a part of Christ's type of religion. Without joining in His concern for the poor, the man couldn't be His disciple. Notice: it was feed the poor first, follow Christ next! What a religion!

Can a 1970s-type man really follow Christ and still be an anti-antipoverty promoter? Has the message of Jesus — "go, sell your possessions, and give to the poor" — changed so that we can live in our comfortable situations and pay no attention to the needs of the poor? Not at all! If you're anti-antipoverty, maybe you'd better check and see if you and Jesus are walking in the same direction.

Notice how simple Christ's antipoverty program is. The "haves" are to sell their possessions and "give the money to the poor" (Williams translation). He assumed that the man could readily identify the have-nots in his society. He said nothing about giving only to poor believers or to the poor whose skin pigmentation matched his or His. It was an unqualified antipoverty program.

Unfortunately, the young man turned Christ's program down by one vote, or should we say veto — not because he didn't believe Jesus to be the sent Messiah — not because he had no concept of who was poor. His personal reasoning was as up-to-date as that of a suburbanite! Plain and simple, he was selfish! He inwardly said, "I've worked hard for what I got, the poor can do the same. What's mine is mine, I'll keep it."

In the nineteen hundred years since the young man's encounter with the Master, few Christians have done much to implement the divine antipoverty program.

To tell the truth, Mr. Reader, how willing are you to follow Christ's suggestion to go sell your possessions and give the money to the poor? Are you man enough to join His antipoverty program? Or will you willingly choose to live as this man — selfish, with a heavy heart, not following Jesus?

Prayer: Lord, I can't boast about keeping all Your commandments, but I desire to walk Your way. Help me, when I see so much poverty in my world, to have compassionate interest toward the poor. Lead me to adopt Your simple antipoverty approach. I pray this realizing that You gave up heaven's riches to become my Saviour, to rescue me from the ultimate in poverty — a bankrupt soul. Amen.

13. WHEN OTHERS DON'T HAVE YOUR LABEL

Scripture: John said to Him, "Teacher, we saw a man using Your name to drive out demons, and we tried to stop him, for he was not one of our followers." Jesus said, "Do not try to stop him; for there is no one who will use my name to do a mighty deed, and then be able soon to abuse me. For whoever is not against us is for us." —*Mark 9:38-40, Williams*

Egotistical, selfish, jealous, exclusive — that's what the disciples were. They saw an outsider doing the same type of ministry they had been commissioned to do and they didn't want him horning in on their domain. Hadn't Jesus given them the power to drive out demons in His name? What right did this outsider have to copy their ministry or cop their power? The man must be stopped — "He was not one of our followers." His robe didn't have the *Made in Jerusalem* brand label. He didn't have the disciples' membership card!

How egotistical men can get in Christ's kingdom! No one can do it like *we* do it. We've obtained a special commissioning from Christ. He called *us* to do this work. Surely there's something wrong if someone else starts doing something similar to our work. We got the idea first. What right have others to copy us? Besides, they aren't *our* followers.

Some men are so proud of their religious labels that they don't contribute much to the kingdom. The label is obvious: Presbyterian, Assembly of God, Church of Christ, Baptist, Methodist, Episcopal. Some make a lot of noise about being nondenominational. Others claim a fundamentalist label. One looks down his nose at the other with an "I'm better than thou" attitude. Rather than joining forces with those of a different denominational brand name, they find fault with the way others perform their ministries. If possible, they downgrade the effectiveness of the other's work. Like the disciples, they boast, "We tried to stop him."

Maybe you're one of these exclusive disciples. You make sure others wear your religious badge or stripe or inside-the-jacket label before you cooperate with them. You make sure a fellow-man's denomination doesn't belong to a certain council of churches before you have fellowship with him. You are suspicious of someone if his church doesn't baptize like your church does it or doesn't stress a particular doctrine or doesn't state a doctrine in the exact language you have memorized. Even if that man says he trusts Jesus as Lord and Saviour, you're not quite sure of his faith. Surely he can't mean the same thing you mean when you make the same statement. He's not one of your followers.

If you've never developed a man-sized faith in Jesus Christ, or made man-sized observations of how the Holy Spirit is at work in the world, the Lord will allow you to maintain your exclusiveness. There are many more of that kind for you to join. But along the way you'll miss some of the pleasure and excitement of seeing God in full operation in society. But that's your choice. You wouldn't think of investigating any other brand name!

Funny how so many twentieth-century Christian men insist on walking a different path than the one trod by the Lord!

Jesus said, "Do not stop him, for there is no one who will use my name to do a mighty deed, and then be able soon to abuse me." No matter whether the other fellow has the same type of church membership certificate, if he's following Jesus, he'll produce Jesus-styled works. If Jesus wasn't afraid that this type of man had the ability to ruin His reputation, why should we be so concerned? If Jesus was willing to accept the outsider as a part of His work in the world, should we not also be as broadminded?

It's spiritually healthy and manly to realize that the work of Christ doesn't rise or fall because of our efforts. Christ has had His witnesses in all ages, in all nations, in all denominations. No matter where or when we might travel, we'll find those who love Christ and who do His work.

Interestingly enough, as someone has said, when we all get to heaven we'll be "united brethren." Why not be manly enough to prepare ourselves upon earth for that eternal label?

Always remember, the other fellow thinks his label is as good as or better than yours. If he didn't, he'd be asking for particulars on how to obtain your brand name!

Thanks be to God who is willing to call us His own no matter who we are, where we live, how much education we have, or what color our skin may be.

Prayer: Lord, forgive me for being so egotistical as to believe that my church or my denomination possesses a special key to Your kingdom. Help me to see that You give out the keys and open the door even to people who seemingly believe the opposite of my pet doctrines. Help me to accept all those whom You have accepted and then work with them whenever and wherever I can until You call it quits. Amen.

14. QUALIFICATIONS OF A STONE THROWER

Scripture: The Bible scholars and the Pharisees brought to Him a woman who had been caught in adultery . . . "Teacher," they told Him, . . . "In the Law, Moses ordered us to stone such a woman. Now, what do You say?" . . . But when they kept asking Him, He got up. "Anyone that's without sin among you," He said, "should be the first to throw a stone at her." — *John 8:3-5, 7, Beck*

Why is it that so many men who are well-versed in the Bible seem to be the quickest to find fault with others? to condemn others? This is as true today in our enlightened Christian era as it was in Jesus' time. In fact, it seems to have gotten worse. It seems that the more people learn about the love of Christ, the less they practice it. What a paradox!

The situation in His day: some Bible scholars and religious leaders became supersnoopers. You'd have to be to *catch* someone committing adultery. That's not a sin that a man and woman commit on the sidewalk. It's also interesting that they caught only the woman having the affair. Why did they let the fellow go free? But isn't that just like men — excuse the sin of a man, but accuse a woman?

As soon as we learn of the sin of another person, the usual reaction is to suggest a severe punishment. We've even thought, "That's what he had coming to him. God always punishes men for their sins." Or in this case, "her." Somehow we get an inner satisfaction out of condemning others who have done wrong.

Admittedly, adultery isn't just a passing fancy. It's a gross sin. It's a sin that a person wilfully commits. If a person is to be punished for it, he has it coming — so we think. Notice how the Bible scholars and Pharisees appealed to the Law of Moses. According to the Law, much like the codes often set up in our churches, the woman should be severely punished.

43

Interestingly enough, some of Christ's antagonists didn't give up. They kept insisting that He come up with a condemnatory answer. They expected Him to agree with them.

How like modern men who often use biblical passages to support their character assassinations, who indulge in condemning everyone who disagrees with them.

But Jesus didn't join their condemnation. He realized that the woman had been caught in an act that demanded punishment by stoning. But He also knew the inner thoughts and the inner motivations of His self-styled righteous listeners. He could have easily told them to fulfill the Law, but He chose rather to challenge their concept of guilt and righteousness and forgiveness. He laid down the qualifications for a stone thrower.

Those qualifications were simple: "Anyone that's without sin among you should be the first to throw a stone at her." Isn't that fair enough? The righteous man ought to have the right to condemn a sinner.

We all know the story — as Jesus continued to write in the sand, all of the religious fellows dropped their rocks and sneaked away. Each one knew he didn't meet the qualifications of a stone thrower. Each one knew of the secret sins that he harbored in his personality. Each one decided that the best way to get out of the situation was to flee. Consequently, since all the accusers disappeared, Jesus dropped the charge against the woman, yet He sternly warned her not to continue in sin.

When we're tempted to condemn someone, especially to verbalize about it in the church or in public, let's bring out Christ's stone thrower's qualifications. It sure would do the church a peck of good. And it might even induce the accused to join up.

The church doesn't need any more stone throwers. It already has far too many. So, even if you know that someone has committed a great sin, drop your stones. There just might be another stone thrower with his arm cocked toward you.

Dropping your stones will do the accused far more good than throwing them. And wouldn't you rather see the glowing face of a forgiven sinner than to be among those with glowering countenances? It's up to you — you know the qualifications. But if you insist on throwing stones, even what Christ says about it doesn't really matter!

Prayer: Lord, give me the grace to judge others exactly as I want to be judged. Also provide the spirit that willingly forgives so that I'll be like Yourself. Here are my stones. Amen.

15. LORD, YOU OFFENDED THEM!

Scripture: Then the disciples came to him and said, "Do you know that the Pharisees have taken great offence at what you have been saying?" — *Matthew 15:12, New English Bible*

Some men are insulted rather quickly. Their skin is thin. They feel picked upon. They think other men are out to get them. They turn even innocent remarks made by others into attacks upon themselves. No matter how careful the speaker might be, he won't avoid having such people take offense at his remarks — especially if he says anything that is significant.

Assuredly, some men seem bent upon insulting and offending others. All their remarks contain some sharp barbs. They play with information — twisting it to entertain themselves, to get a laugh out of friends, or to deliberately tear down the reputations of others.

But there are the Pharisee-types who are offended when their true characters are revealed. The Pharisees had attacked Jesus' disciples' so-called breaking of the sabbath — they didn't wash their hands before eating! He insulted them by asking them, "Why do you break God's commandment in the interest of your tradition?" They were more concerned in fulfilling their traditions than they were in fulfilling the law's demands through love. Jesus further added insult to injury by truthfully pointing out that they made God's law null and void by their practices.

Wow! No wonder the disciples later told Jesus, "Don't You know You offended them?"

If you're offended by the statements of others, whom do you blame? The Pharisees surely didn't look inward — they never did. Do you? Surely it wouldn't be right to accept guilt for being offended, especially when someone as opposed to you as Jesus was opposed to the Pharisees makes an offending statement.

Knowing what we know about the Pharisees, we say the fault was totally theirs. Surely Jesus shouldn't be accused of making insulting remarks. We don't correlate insulting remarks with the purity of His character. The sinless Saviour wouldn't be guilty of impure remarks. No, the guilt was not His. Being insulted is an inward problem — one we would accuse the Pharisees of having.

But with us, it's the other fellow's fault. He makes the insulting remarks. He offends. He's guilty. He'd better change.

That's the easy way to cover up the inward problems that come quickly to the surface when someone makes an insulting remark. But it's not the manly way to solve the issue. If you're offended by what others say, check the inward reasons. Maybe even the remarks of Christ would offend you. If they do, then there's need of some drastic action.

In a world that has so many problems of its own, there's no place for a follower of Jesus Christ to be wearing his feelings on his sleeve. There is a great need for us men to check out the reasons we get offended, confess these reasons to the Lord in earnest prayer, and then determine to live in such a way that others are drawn to Christ through our lives.

Yes, it's easy to be offended. But that isn't the way to show that you're a maturing man and a maturing Christian. If your religion is still on your sleeve, there's some good evidence that it isn't much deeper.

Prayer: I admit that I've been too touchy. Remarks by others have hurt my feelings. I've avoided some people because I don't like their sharp words. First of all, give me a thicker skin if it will help me to maintain communication with those who seem bent on verbally tearing others or even me apart. And if I am deliberately offending others, give me that spirit of Jesus that loves. If the offense is within my personality, help me to grow up. Take from my life those things that aren't right, that have been touchy areas in my soul. Amen.

16. LOOKING FOR EASY SOLUTIONS

Scripture: He saw a great crowd waiting, and His heart was moved with pity at the sight of them, for they were like sheep without a shepherd . . . His disciples came to Him and said . . . "Send the crowds off to the farms and villages to buy themselves something to eat." But He answered them, "Give them something to eat yourselves." — *Mark 6:34-37, Williams*

If only there had been an entrepreneur among the five thousand dusty-footed followers of Jesus on that day, he'd have made a mint. Muttonburgers or fishsticks would have tasted good along about evening — and a camel-drawn snack wagon would have alleviated the problem facing the disciples. Now why didn't someone think of the money they could have made by following the itinerant Jesus around the Galilean region? Unfortunately, the slow-paced, sheep-tending Jews hadn't heard about American fast-food franchises.

Besides, the disciples had a much better method for solving the gigantic problem of feeding over five thousand hungry people. And it seems that many followers of Jesus Christ still prefer the disciples' philosophy concerning meeting the needs of mankind. The disciples simply said (much the same way many middle-class Americans state their ideas about helping the poor), "Let them go and find their own food."

Somehow, most people who "have made it" believe that everyone else can make it. The disciples had enough money for their own food. They weren't responsible if others in the crowd lacked the foresight to bring along at least a sack lunch. They didn't sense the responsibility for the hungry stomachs of the multitudes, not even the crying children who must have been tugging at their parents' clothing. The easiest way to solve the problem was to let each individual satisfy his own hunger pangs. Why should they shoulder this responsibility?

There's always an easy solution to the problems of others. Simply send them away to solve problems in their own manner whether they have the capacity or resources to do it or not. That's the way many Christians propose that America solve its ghetto and race problems. Let the poor and the blacks come up with adequate solutions — like the middle-class whites did several years ago. By saying the problems aren't ours, we can shun any moral or financial responsibility. It's their problem, let them find the solutions!

A second easy answer to problems is simply to pretend that the problems don't exist. This wasn't the disciples' approach, but it's a common one. If we avoid driving through a ghetto we soon convince ourselves that such places don't exist. If we have no contact with those who go to bed hungry every night, we forget that they exist. We can go about being involved in building our own homes or feeding our own families to the extent that we do not hear the wails of the hungry multitudes.

A third easy answer to problems is to substitute our problems for the problems of others. This the disciples did when they carefully explained to Jesus that they had only forty dollars. How much food would that buy? He must have been kidding when He told them to go and purchase food for five thousand!

You've probably told someone who was bemoaning his lot in life, "Don't tell me your problems, I have enough of my own." And when you don't want to get involved in finding solutions to others' problems, you invent a few problems of your own.

Sure, Jesus was a miracle performer. Yet He had the same options as those open to the disciples. He could have sent the crowds away to find their own food. He could have avoided any embarrassment to the disciples. He could have made it easier for Himself by sidestepping the situation. But He didn't — and consequently five thousand people went away not only well fed, but as ambassadors to tell what Christ had done.

Not that we want the needy to go around telling how great we are, but to demonstrate that the compassion of Christ has permeated our souls, we need to face problems head on. He who would always find an easy solution isn't really a man at all!

Prayer: Jesus, how great to know that You never sidestepped any problems. Forgive me for being so much like your first disciples. Give me the courage and wisdom to seek solutions to the great needs others face in my community, in the ghetto, in all the world. I pray that Your problem-solving compassion may possess my entire personality. Amen.

17. OFF THE TOP OF YOUR HEAD

Scripture: He took Peter and John and James with him, and went up onto the mountain side to pray. And even as he prayed, the fashion of his face was altered. . . . Meanwhile, Peter and his companions were sunk in sleep; and they awoke to see him in his glory, and the two men standing with him. . . . Peter said to Jesus, Master, it is well that we should be here; let us make three booths in this place, one for thee, and one for Moses, and one for Elias. But he spoke at random. . . . — *Luke 9:28, 29, 32, 33, Knox*

Deacon Clarence fell asleep every Sunday about ten minutes into the sermon. He usually woke up just as the pastor announced the closing hymn and said, "Let us stand to sing."

One Sunday the pastor got extremely excited in his pulpiteering. About halfway through the sermon he shouted, "If anyone here would like to go to hell, please stand up!"

The sleepy deacon heard the "stand up" so he popped up. Suddenly he noticed that he was the only pewsitter standing. He looked around and then blurted out, "I don't know what we're voting for, but pastor, it looks like you and I are the only ones for it!"

The other pewsitters laughed. Clarence sat down. His "off the top of his head" remark made him exceedingly embarrassed.

Luke tells us that the disciple Peter had a similar nonthinking experience. He says that Peter "spoke at random" — without definite purpose, haphazardly, without adequate thought.

Peter, along with James and John, had experienced the tail end of the Transfiguration. They got in on just the conclusion of a glorious happening. Unfortunately, because they missed the earlier encounter with Moses and Elijah, they didn't have much of a basis for making any statements. But in typical style, Peter talked off the top of his head. He made an on-the-spot proposal: let's set up three worship booths — one representing the Law by Moses; one representing the prophets through Elijah; and one, of course, for Christ.

How much like Peter are you? Do you speak up on almost every occasion simply because you get the inner urge to say something? Do you ever apologize by saying, "Just off the top of my head, I'd say . . ." and then spill forth some high sounding theory or proposed action without taking into account the full scope of the situation?

Such at random thinking has to be tolerated in the church much more than in business. A business firm's personnel soon detects the shallowness of such proposals and gets wise to the proponent. Some men even get fired as a result of "top of the head" proposals that fail. But in the church, others usually grin and bear it.

Unfortunate is the man, who, like Peter, doesn't understand his mental predicament. Peter didn't realize he was talking off the top of his head. He was momentarily convinced that his proposal was one of the greatest ideas he had ever originated. He gave no thought to the fact that his proposal might be out of line with Christ's thinking.

The church is overcrowded with men who talk off the tops of their heads. Even pulpiteers are guilty. Rather than giving issues mind-taxing consideration, we simply talk about them. That's why the world often doesn't take the church seriously. We really don't have any concrete answers to the pressing problems around us. We're still talking off the tops of our heads. That's much easier than research and development. And besides, such talk usually remains in the talk stage — we don't have to roll up our sleeves or make any sacrificial donations when talking at random.

It's doubtful whether Peter ever fully learned the discipline of thinking before talking. He had a few later experiences where his tongue did his thinking. And in each case he had to learn the truth the hard way.

It's often been said, "Some people only learn the hard way." To talk off the top of your head and then be rebuked for such loose-lipped thinking is indeed a difficult way to learn. Here's hoping that the activity of your tongue will follow the activity of your brain — not vice versa. You and the world around you will be better off because of it.

Prayer: Lord, develop in me the character that knows how to logically think through a subject before I make any verbal proposals. Keep my tongue from being in high gear while my brain is still in neutral. Help me to maintain a cranial guard over my voice box. Amen.

18. THAT ISN'T THE WAY WE DO IT

Scripture: The Pharisees and some Bible scholars who had come from Jerusalem gathered around Jesus. They saw some of His disciples eat with unclean hands, that is, without washing them. (Now the Pharisees, like all other Jews, don't eat without washing their hands up to the wrist — to keep the rules handed down by their fathers . . . and there are many other rules they've learned to keep — baptizing cups, pitchers, copper pans, couches.) "Why don't Your disciples live according to the rules handed down by our fathers?" — *Mark 7:1-5, Beck*

In a church where the elements of the Lord's Supper are distributed among the seated congregation by the deacons, a young minister once passed the cups first, then the broken bread. His mistake was brought on by the misplacing of the trays on the communion table. The deaconesses had placed the bread trays close to the edge. The young minister, standing too close to the table, reached over the bread trays and took the cups first. One deacon almost stopped the minister, but thought, "He has a habit of doing things differently, so why stop him."

Among the church members was a retired minister's wife. She whispered (loud enough to be heard by almost a third of the congregation), "I've never seen it done that way before!"

Tradition, much like the handwashing rules of the Pharisees, had bound her to such an extent that she didn't realize that even the gospels record the fact that Jesus distributed the supper elements "backwards." Read the enlightening text—Luke 22:14-20.

Whether it's backward distribution of the Lord's Supper elements, a proposed change in the worship service, a new Christian education approach, a youthful expression of how things ought to be done in church, a suggested community outreach — you've heard others say it, possibly you've said it yourself, "That isn't the way we do it!"

For some reason we fear change. It's much easier to live according to traditions. If nothing changes, we can go from day to day without doing much thinking to answer the challenges made to our traditions. We can maintain a subtle smugness that says everything is right as it is. We can even feel quite pious about how successful we have been in maintaining the status quo or in meeting all the rules of our particular denomination or nondenomination.

Suddenly there has arisen in the church a generation of upstarts, who in the language of the Pharisees and Bible scholars of Jesus' day, "eat with unclean hands, that is, without washing them . . . up to the wrists." They've decided that the traditions are a lot of bunk. Just because the elders do it according to tradition, the youth have decided there's another way. Who says traditions are holy? Who says the rules of the past cannot be changed or even broken? Who says we can't change the practices and still maintain the faith — or even purify it and make it more believable and practical?

It all depends on a man's attitude toward his faith! If you insist on being a defender of the faith; if you believe that what your church says about the Bible is as holy as what the Bible itself says; if you believe that change means compromise; if your personal religion is more of an adherence to traditions and rules than it is a personal friendship with Jesus; if you must express your religion in cliched ways — you'll maintain the Pharisaic philosophy. You'll be sure to propagate the many other rules you've learned to keep. You'll insist, as did the "Bible scholars" of Christ's era, that people ought to "live according to the rules handed down by our fathers."

If you're a real man, a man that can sift out the tradition of men from the truths of Christ, you'll see a lot of good in doing things in an unorthodox manner. You'll see that change in approach in no way threatens previously held doctrines. You'll see that fresh methods enhance the presentation of the gospel. You'll enjoy your relationship to Christ because it'll take on a less stilted form. You'll be an inspiration to those whose traditions haven't been as inbred as yours.

Unfortunately a great number of your fellow men in the church won't become real men. They'll keep insisting that you have to do it their way or else you won't be accepted in the group. Be of good cheer, the early followers of Jesus had the same problems. In fact, the nonconformist Jesus had to go it alone most of the time. So if you break with tradition, if others say "we don't do it that way," fear not nor apologize, you're in the best of company!

Prayer: Lord, give me the power to differentiate between what is tradition and what is truth, then help me to express the truth in a manner consistent with myself and in harmony with Your ways of operating in our world. If, perchance, this goes against set patterns in the church, may I be man enough to stand on my own. Amen.

19. WHAT DO YOU DO ON SUNDAYS?

Scripture: On another sabbath day it happened that he went into the synagogue to teach, when there was a man there who had his right hand withered. The scribes and Pharisees were watching him, to see whether he would restore health on the sabbath . . . Jesus said to them, I have a question to ask you; which is right, to do good on the sabbath day, or to do harm? — *Luke 6:6, 7, 9, Knox*

If only Jesus would have minded His own business, we'd have the perfect example of what a man ought to do on Sundays. Luke tells us that on that particular sabbath "it happened that He went into the synagogue to teach." That sounds great. In fact, we place a great deal of importance upon Him as the Master Teacher. We also like to pride ourselves in our weekly teaching sessions at the local church. Is not this following the Master's example?

54

If only Christ would have spent all of His time presenting the gospel. If He hadn't spent so much time helping the needy, healing the sick, doing good deeds — especially on the sabbath days (the seventh day in those days, Sunday to us moderns). If . . . then it would be easy to determine what to do on Sundays. In fact, it would solve a few other problems that face us in this socially oriented society. Some people would be exceedingly happy if Jesus was *only* a gospeler. They could bury their heads between the black covers of a Scofield Bible and come up with weekly expositions of eternal truths. But, unfortunately for such people, Jesus just doesn't fit that pattern.

It's true, Jesus did enter the synagogue on that particular sabbath to teach. But we're never told whether He presented anything from the Scriptures, how much He expounded eternal truths, or how long He preached that day. Maybe all the teaching He accomplished was wrapped up in His encounter with the withered-handed man and the violent reactions of His critics.

But what did He do on that sabbath? He saw a man in need. He supplied a remedy to that need before He presented any theological information. He based His teaching upon the encounter He had at that moment.

What a contrast to most of our Sundays! We even print little cliches in church bulletins, such as, "Enter to worship, leave to serve"; or "When the worship ends, the service begins." Jesus did this in reverse. He made sure He got His service in right at the beginning.

What would happen to your Sunday worship if you had to find an opportunity to help someone? Would you ever make it to church? Would you need a late-late service — after you've had all day to find some needy person? Would you have to forget the worship end of the deal?

Unfortunately too many modern men would rather argue about what should or shouldn't be done on Sunday. They'd rather criticize others who are doing something; they'd rather make sarcastic remarks about desecrating the sabbath! Some like to make loud references to what God did after six days of creative work.

Some like to lounge around — to "rest" like the Creator did. They forget that God was in Christ — thus giving a new dimension not only to what Christian teaching is all about, but demonstrating that the most powerful lessons are transmitted through particular applications of truth.

If your Sundays are simply days in which you spend hours absorbing what others teach and preach; if your Sundays are wrapped up only in church attendance, relaxation at home, and more church attendance — why not take another look at what the Master did on His day at the local synagogue? Don't brag if your Sundays don't contain some activities that might cause you to soil your hands by reaching out to needy people.

It can become a dangerous way of living if you put service before sanctimonious singing — but you're in good company. That Person standing beside you has nail prints in His hands!

Prayer: Forgive me for being Pharisaic in my attitudes toward Sunday. Help me to remember Your words, "Man was not made for the sabbath, but the sabbath for man." Help me always to do good to those in need — regardless of what day of the week it might be. Amen

20. SO YOU'VE SURRENDERED ALL!

Scripture: Then Peter spoke up: "Look! We gave up everything and followed You." "Let Me assure you," Jesus said, "everyone who gave up his home, brothers and sisters, mother, father, or children, or fields for Me and for the good news, will certainly get a hundred times as much here in this life: houses, brothers and sisters, mothers and children and fields, with persecutions, and in the coming world everlasting life." — *Mark 10:28-30, Beck*

You remember Christ's call to the unpolished, unvarnished fishermen. He saw Peter tending his fishing gear and said, "Follow me and I'll make you a fisher of men."

Peter seemingly understood. He dropped the fishy-smelling line and nets and followed Jesus. One can readily sense the pleasure Christ must have had in making such a quick catch.

The word got around. Peter had forsaken all to follow Jesus. In fundamentalist parlance, Peter was completely separated. When the chorus sang, "Is your all on the altar of sacrifice laid?" Peter answered in his rough baritone voice, "I surrender all!"

But there comes a time in every man's life when his verbal commitments are challenged, when his life has to defend his lip. Peter was no exception when Jesus described the difficulty some would have in entering the kingdom. Some held on to their riches and prestige. These kept them outside.

But Peter's piety had to express itself. Already he had developed a better-than-those attitude. He tugged at the Master's shoulder and said, "Look here, Jesus. We gave up everything to follow You."

Some, like Peter, pride themselves in how much they have given up to follow Jesus. A talented businessman is converted. He gives up (always by choice or sometimes because he can't stand the former conditions) a large salary and "sacrifices" to join a religious organization. Then others keep repeating the story, "Look how much he's given up to work for the Lord."

It's so easy to keep reminding Christ what we've given up to follow Him. "Look, Lord, we've given up everything to follow You." We do this to bolster our standing with the Lord. We do it to cover up something we really haven't surrendered. We do it to impress those who hear our testimony. We do it to have leverage in asking the Lord to grant a request. We do it to maintain a comfortable inner feeling.

Only the foolhardy will repeat Peter's phrases. An honest man will constantly find areas of life that are self-dominated rather than Christ-controlled. Sure it sounds good to sing, "All to Jesus I surrender, all to Him I freely give." But is it true? Have we gone the ultimate distance in surrender? If we have, it's unusual. And it's even more unusual not to remind the Lord, ourselves, or others that we have committed ourselves, and all that is labeled, "ours" to divine directorship and ownership.

Usually the man who approaches a 99 percent Lord-controlled life doesn't believe he's anywhere near that point. He'd be the last to make such a proclamation. He's usually too busy doing what the Lord wants done in the world to realize his personal piety. When he takes time out to consider his relative position before the Lord, he appeals for mercy, pardon, acceptance, direction. He seeks to allow Christ new inroads into his personality. And if he ever mentions giving up anything, he does it apologetically in his prayer closet, not in the public assembly of believers.

The problem most of us modern men have is that we're too much like Peter and not enough like Jesus. We want everyone to know what we've given up to follow the Lord. We want the public to know how much it has cost us to be Christians. We're too conscious of our image in the community.

So you've surrendered everything?

Prayer: Lord, forgive me for boasting of my personal sacrificing on Your account. Give me a fuller understanding of humble, tight-lipped commitment of my personality and possessions to You and Your causes. I need so much to accept a fuller measure of Your directorship and ownership of my life and substance. Supply the will power to surrender more. Amen.

21. RUNNING ERRANDS FOR JESUS

Scripture: After this, when he was approaching Bethphage and Bethany, close to the mountain which is called Olivet, he sent two of his disciples on an errand; Go into the village that faces you, he told them, and as you enter it you will find a colt tethered there, one on which no man has yet ridden; untie it and bring it here. And if anybody asks you, Why are you untying it? this must be your answer, The Lord has need of it. — *Luke 19:29-32, Knox*

Errands are experiences upon which we like to send other people; but we often get upset if they are demanded of us. We've come to limit the meaning of this word to some small tasks that are necessary, but usually not too important. We don't usually call going to the bank to deposit $15,000 "an errand." Nor would a farm implement dealer consider delivering a self-propelled combine "running an errand to a farmer down the road."

An errand boy is usually the lowest paid and most dispensable employee of a company. You can always hire a new errand boy. And if, five minutes before quitting time, you have a menial task to be performed, you call the errand boy. He can't say No — he has no authority; anyone can give him orders.

So to be sent on an errand isn't a high-sounding task. It's a servant's job at best. And the end result, although it is necessary, isn't momentous.

When we read that Jesus sent two of His disciples on an errand, we might answer, "What's so significant about that?" Were they sent on the errand because no one else could or would go? Were they sent on an errand that had little importance? Were they happy to comply? It would be interesting to know the names of these two disciples. Would Peter and Judas Iscariot be willing to be errand boys — especially to go fetch a kicking colt?

The instructions to the two errand disciples were simple —

simple enough for any errand boy. He simply told them to go to the next town and find an unridden colt. They'd find the colt tied. They were to untie it and bring it to Jesus. And if someone asked why they were taking the untamed animal, their answer was simply to be, "The Lord has need of it."

The two disciples performed their errand well. They even repeated the magic words that allowed them to take the colt with no additional words or securities. And what seemed like an insignificant errand, except for a few kickings by the colt, became a part of a significant event. Jesus rode on the colt into Jerusalem as a victorious king. Did those two disciples consider themselves on a "minor errand" at the time they followed Jesus' instructions? If so, they must have been chagrined over the memory of this attitude when, in later years, they recalled their part in the triumphal entry.

Twentieth-century men have especially to reexamine their willingness to run errands for Jesus. How many times have tasks seemed insignificant? How many times have others in His kingdom asked us to do what seemed exceedingly menial? How often have we considered our tasks unimportant or subordinate when we should have looked upon them as a service to Christ?

If we can't do errands in the kingdom of God, we're not really men. We're less than robust. We have an ego problem. We believe that we are more than what either Christ or others consider us to be. We believe that we ought to be recognized because of our talents or status and then be given jobs accordingly. Why should we waste our well-developed talents doing the insignificant? If we're the most educated in the church, why should we be asked to work on clean-up day? If we possess the most glorious voice in the congregation, why should we sing in the Sunday school primary department? If we have such dynamic speaking abilities, why should we be asked to teach the rowdy junior boys? We've got all this talent, why-oh-why isn't it being used properly?

We can miss much of the dynamic of Christian living simply by waiting to do something big for the Lord. We can miss most of the joy Christ promised to the believers, if we are bound by high opinions of ourselves. The humble person who is anxious to run errands for Jesus is the one who gives evidence of inner joy. Such a person isn't concerned about personal reputation or glory; he knows there's a task to be done for the Lord and he simply must pitch in to accomplish it.

A man's willingness to run errands in the kingdom of Christ is in direct relationship to his willingness to be a servant. A true servant doesn't really care how large or how small the service may be. He's only interested in serving.

How about you? Would you run errands for Jesus if He asked? Or do you feel the necessity of being the one to give the orders? The kingdom advances more by those who fulfill the errands than those who plan to move mountains. Don't be afraid of being an errand boy for the Lord. You just might be involved in preparing things for His second triumphal entry!

Prayer: Lord, help me to consider no service insignificant. Help me to see all tasks from Your perspective. And when You command, give me the inner spirit that will respond with, "Here am I, send me." Help me to say this with meaning right off, regardless of the task. Amen.

22. LET ME DO THIS FIRST

Scripture: To another he said, Follow me, and he answered, Lord, give me leave to go home and bury my father first. But Jesus said to him, Leave the dead to bury their dead; it is for thee to go out and proclaim God's kingdom. And there was yet another who said, Lord, I will follow thee, but first let me take leave of my friends. To him Jesus said, No one who looks behind him, when he has once put his hand to the plough, is fitted for the kingdom of God. — *Luke 9:59-62, Knox*

A real man rarely gives excuses! He responds to challenges with a resounding Yes or a definite No. But such real manly fellows seem to be rare. Why?

Luke tells us about two non-manly fellows. The first one seemed to have a legitimate reason, rather than an excuse, for not following Jesus right off. But let's analyze.

If his father had just died, why was he in the crowd that was following Jesus? Why wasn't he at the funeral director's place of business making arrangements for the last rites? In that era, very little time lapsed between the time of death and the hour of burial. In most cases the man would have utilized most of his extra time (after making proper burial arrangements) in engaging in a sort of "show and tell" mourning. Why was he out with the crowd? Probably because his father was still alive. Probably he simply had made up his mind that if he was going to follow Jesus, it would be at a time most convenient to his personal circumstances. At that hour he needed a handy excuse to bypass Christ's challenge for immediate fellowship!

We can more readily understand Christ's answer if we look at the man's statement from the perspective of its superficiality. One can't take the Saviour literally here. It's impossible for a dead man to bury another dead man. Jesus wouldn't have made such a foolish suggestion. He was a most practical man!

Too often the excuses we give to get ourselves off the hook of responsibility toward God or toward others ring with the same type of illogical superficiality. Think back to the last ten so-called reasons you gave to get out of doing some task at church. How many were as pathetic as this man's excuse? How many would stand the test of logic? How many could you honestly repeat with a straight face? How many would you have readily accepted if they were offered to you by others?

The pathetic part of the man's reasoning was that he felt his excuse was sufficiently important for him to be dismissed from a God-stated task — a task that should have been even more important to the man than burying his father. His self-delusion was not too much different than that of some men in today's world.

One further comment about his excuse. He used one he thought would be beyond attack. Who would attack a man's concern about such a grave subject? Who would dare to say there was anything more important than the proper burial of a loved one? Who would have the nerve to challenge a man's right to making proper funeral arrangements? But he forgot one thing — he wasn't dealing with an ordinary man!

The second man's excuse wasn't very cleverly stated. It appeared flippant — possibly even to the man himself. He had to go say Good-bye to all his friends — as if they really cared whether he followed Jesus. Since Christ had been ministering in the area, and since the country was quite small, he could have easily gotten back home on occasion to say Hello or Good-bye to his friends. They probably wouldn't have noticed that he was gone, and if they did, they would probably keep in touch through his parents.

Again it was the priority given to the less meaningful when the most meaningful loomed so large before him. He chose the trivial when the tremendous was open to him. He gave an excuse simply because he didn't want to comply with the demands that following Christ would impose on him.

No wonder Jesus said, "No one who looks behind him, when he has once put his hand to the plough is fitted for the kingdom of God." The fellow who isn't full-hearted in his commitment, who offers excuses, isn't fit for the kingdom. The fellow who finds the insignificant more important than the significant isn't the "I surrender all" type that Christ desires.

"Let me do this first" is not the theory of Christ's kingdom. He wants primary loyalty. He wants full allegiance.

Have you ever offered an excuse in order to evade some responsibility in Christ's kingdom? If you have, don't criticize these two fellows. Admit you're No. 3!

But don't despair. To get into the kingdom column, just stop making excuses. Besides, you'll find that the reasons for keeping your hands to the plough are much more satisfying and exciting than any worked-out excuse could ever be.

Prayer: Lord, give me an honest heart to say Yes or No to the divine demands put upon my life. Strip away the hypocrisy that offers excuses. Lead me to such a point of yieldedness that I am not tempted to turn back from following You because of the attraction of secondary issues of life. Amen.

23. A LESSON IN PRAYER

Scripture: Once Jesus was praying in a certain place. When He stopped, one of His disciples asked Him, "Lord, teach us to pray as John taught his disciples." He told them, "When you pray, say Father, may Your name be kept holy, Your kingdom come, Your will be done on earth as it is in heaven. Give us every day our daily bread. Forgive us our sins, as we, too, forgive everyone who sins against us. And don't bring us into temptation." — *Luke 11:1-4, Beck*

Have you ever asked anyone to teach you to pray? Have you ever studied a series of lessons on prayer in Sunday school? Has your pastor ever zeroed in on teaching prayer techniques?

Most of us have been schooled in the importance of prayer. Pastors have preached about it. Friends have told us they are praying for us. Church services begin and end with prayer and have at least two prayers in between. When faced with a big crisis or decision, you've been glad when someone told you they'd remember you in prayer. And when the crisis came, you prayed!

One modern translation states their request thus, "Lord, teach us how to pray." The others simply say, "teach us to pray." Let's start with the first.

"Teach us *how* to pray." Teach us the techniques of prayer. What kind of words ought we use? How should we address the Father? Should a man also pray directly to Christ and to the Holy Spirit? Should we quote Bible verses in prayer? What does the Bible say about techniques in prayer? Should we use "Thee" and "Thou" when addressing God, or may we use the language of today? Would God be insulted if we called Him "You"?

Such questions lead a man into the techniques of prayer. They help a man formulate the words and ideas he addresses heavenward. They lead him into subjects of interest that he can share with deity.

After listening to most people pray, one might conclude there are a collection of cliches that God especially likes to — or else must — hear constantly. The average public prayer meeting contains prayers that are loaded with these worn-out expressions. It almost appears that to be acceptable to God — and certain church fellowships — one must learn a specific vocabulary.

Learning techniques that will keep prayer on a fresh, vital, present-day level of conversation with God is most valuable. How refreshing to talk to God as a Friend. How exciting to know that God understands a man's everyday words. This type of prayer demands that a man learn some personalized techniques — techniques that are totally his own. This is the *how* prayer. And one can be assured that in an intimate relationship with Jesus Christ, the Lord will direct in how we pray.

But there's another approach. This does not deal with the wording of our prayers. This deals with motivation. One can

possess good techniques for praying, but not pray. One can understand what language to use in addressing God, but if he does not
use it in actual communication with God, it has little value. And
although the prayer that Jesus taught His disciples seems to be
heavily slanted toward the content features, there's good evidence
the disciples could have been asking about motivation after ob-
serving that John the Baptist's followers knew how to pray and
must have been known for praying.

"Teach us to pray." Give us that inner motivation to pray. The
average man needs that inner push that gets him to open his mind
and mouth heavenward. He needs that energy that draws him into
a conversation with God.

How do we get motivation to pray? We can't learn it as we
could learn the techniques of prayer. We can't get it by listening
to others, especially to those who mouth the cliches. We can't get
it by reading books on prayer or books of prayers. Motivation has
to come from the Holy Spirit. He has to invade our inner personality. He has to take over the control of our living. He has to
inspire us to a personal contact with the Father. He has to lead
us into daily conversation with Christ.

Yet, even this is a subtly fleeting thing unless we are constantly
aware of the work of the Holy Spirit. We have to submit to His
leadership, life-changing work, and creativity. Motivation becomes much a matter of will — ours submitted to His.

Remember, the fellows who asked Jesus to teach them to pray
weren't sissies. They were rough men — men who often trusted
their own strength. But how inspiring is the thought that they
sought both the techniques and motivation to speak intelligently
and challengingly to God. Let us also seek.

Prayer that has fresh content; prayer that is motivated by the
thrust of your inner devotion and need; prayer that is the expression of your present thinking and feeling toward God — that's
what this business of praying is all about. Let us pray!

Prayer: Lord, I've prayed too often just with words, words, words.
I've used too many churchy cliches. Inspire me to say what I
mean and mean what I say. Amen.

66

24. SAYING "WHAT DO YOU MEAN?" TO GOD

Scripture: Now while everybody was wondering at all that He was doing, He said to His disciples, "You must store away in your memories these words, for the Son of Man is going to be turned over to thousands of men!" But they remained ignorant of what this meant; indeed, it had been hidden from them, so that they did not grasp it, and they were afraid to ask Him about this statement. — *Luke 9:43-45, Williams*

The junior high school girl almost failed the science course even though she was a rather good student. It wasn't a matter of brain power. She almost failed because she was too timid to ask the science teacher questions when she didn't understand some aspect of the scientific experiments. She kept quiet when she should have raised her hand and asked, "What do you mean?"

Now, it's true that a lot of men remain ignorant of the purposes of God for their lives and in the world for far different reasons, but some never seem to be bold enough to ask Him, "What do You mean?"

Many men remain ignorant of the purposes of God because they rarely study His textbook. They set the course of their own lives with little or no difficulty and don't feel any necessity for consulting the Word of God. If they were ever asked to give a biblical basis for their faith or for their actions, they'd turn embarrassingly red. Or else they'd excuse themselves or question whether one could really turn to the Bible for some specific text that would spell out how a man ought to act in a twentieth-century situation. We've all heard someone say, "The Bible doesn't say anything about going to the moon," etc.

For some men to consult the Bible for guidance is to admit an inner weakness. They'd rather go it alone. Or perhaps they've accepted the eternal benefits of believing some Bible verses, but they don't want to be restrained by other verses. They just aren't manly enough to open themselves up to the full implications of the Word of God. They just aren't manly enough to allow the Holy Spirit to give God's answer to the circumstances of their lives.

In direct contrast to these attitudes are the attitudes expressing God's side of the situation. Jesus said, "Ask and you will receive." James wrote, "If any of you lack wisdom, let him ask of God." So the invitation seems clear: if a man doesn't quite understand what the Lord seems to be saying in a particular situation, he should ask for an explanation.

If you remain ignorant of the will of God for your life, there's a good possibility it's willful ignorance. The man who searches out the mind of God, through prayer and a thorough study of the Bible, will be able to determine the Lord's plan. In many cases it's simply a matter of asking.

Then there are those sticky situations. Possibly the disciples faced this type in this episode described by Luke. They couldn't figure out what their Master meant. Such types of situations shouldn't inspire fear, but faith. In such situations the Lord is especially desirous to explain what He means. In fact, He seems more willing to explain and to divulge the secrets of the sticky situations than the more obvious ones. Possibly He leaves the more obvious ones for us to figure out ourselves. He who created the human mind not only knows its capacities but also how it will function under each type of pressure. And in many cases that's how He wants it.

God is open to the questions of any man. He hears us at any hour of the day. He never turns a deaf ear to our words. He doesn't clobber us simply because we have questioning minds. In fact it would seem that God invites the questioner since He invented the possibility of questioning. He delights in satisfying the hearts of men. If you come in a truly inquiring spirit, God will come to you in kind understanding.

Perchance even then the answer doesn't come. Perchance the crisis comes upon us and we don't know what the will of God is because the Bible seems silent to us. Perchance the answer to our *Why?* question does not come when we ask. Is God answering our inquiry? Yes, but in a manner known only to Himself. Maybe the best answer is the one of silence. Maybe this kind of answer makes us more of the man God wants us to be. Maybe this reaction from heaven draws us into a better understanding of the complexity of the answers that God must give to the world because He sees situations not simply from the present-day viewpoint, but from an eternal perspective. Maybe the silent answer is necessary for the completion of His plan in the months, years, or even decades to come. That's why He keeps the channels open so we can ask Him questions. Always remember, God satisfies the inquiring mind and He specializes in clearing up fuzzy thinking.

Prayer: Give me the humility to admit there are thousands of things that I don't know. Then give me the courage to go to the One who really knows everything. May my knowledge of Your purposes increase. But along with this, may I have the willingness to fit into those purposes that I already understand. Amen.

25. IF YOU COULD MAKE ONLY ONE REQUEST

Scripture: A leper came up to Him, and prostrated himself before Him, and said, "Lord, if you choose to, you can cure me." Then He put out His hand and touched him, and said, "I do choose to, be cured." And at once his leprosy was cured. — *Matthew 8:2, 3, Williams*

If you had an incurable disease, such as this leper's slow-death malady, it's easy to tell what your one request would be. This leper couldn't conceive of anything greater that could happen to him than that he be cured. So he threw himself down at Jesus' feet and cried. "Cure me!" Fame or fortune wouldn't have eliminated the rot that was slowly dissipating his energy and life. To request happiness or honor would have been meaningless. How could he be happy when he knew he was dying? How could he obtain honor in a society in which he would always remain an outcast?

You don't have leprosy, so what's the significance of this text in your life? Consider for a moment — or will you need a day — or better yet, an entire month — what would you ask for if you could make only one major request?

A struggling businessman might ask for success. Health he already has, but somehow the security and the extra profits that would make the business worthwhile have escaped him. Profits have been too slim to compensate for all the headaches of being in business. "Lord, give me success, that's all I want," he prays. But then he begins to think — is this the ultimate request?

The newly married man hopes that marriage is the fulfillment of his choicest dreams. Even though he has seen other marriages hit the rocks or become endurance contests between one male and one female, *his* marriage will be happy. He and his bride will show the world that they have the secret. They shall live happily ever after. But to assure this, he prays, "Lord, let happiness be ours, that's all I want." But then he begins to think — is this the ultimate request?

The recently elected senator knows that without political acumen he'll exert little influence upon his constituency. They have elected him to the high office for their good. He has become a politician, or better yet a satesman, to do the greatest good. Thus the Christian politician desires to represent both Christ and his constituents in the national government. Torn between statesmanship and political position, the Christian politician prays, "Lord, help me to be a statesman. Let leadership be my portion, that's all I want." But then he too begins to think — is this the ultimate request?

Businessman, newly married man, politician, or whatever you might be — laborer, farmer, company executive, white- or blue-collar worker, self-employed worker or union member — how would you form your ultimate request? Would you follow the pattern of King Solomon and ask for wisdom? God can give that. Would you pray the prayer of Jabez — the only thing we know about him in Scripture — "Wilt Thou grant me a true blessing and extend my boundaries; let Thy hand be with me, and keep calamity from me so that no pain assails me" (I Chronicles 4:10, Berkeley)? God could answer that type of prayer. He did for Jabez. Would you pray the "cure me" cry of the leper? God answered that one, too.

Would the most important prayer in your life be in the words of the publican who didn't even lift up his eyes, but smote upon his breast as he cried, "God be merciful to me a sinner"? God answered that prayer.

Some declare that the publican-type prayer is the most important prayer any man can utter. It brings even the manliest type of fellow into a right relationship with Jesus. If you haven't prayed this prayer, you really aren't man enough to stand up to your sins and stand before the Almighty. What's keeping you back?

Formulating life's most important prayer isn't an easy task. For those who face life/death situations, words are almost automatic. But for the rest of us, knowing what is most important in life — the thing we want God to do for us above all else — that isn't easy to decide. What is most important to you might not apply to the man next in line. You can't decide for him, and he can't decide for you. It's only in your man-to-Man relationship to Jesus Christ, when you look Him straight in the eye and He does the same to you, that you will ever determine what's most important. Then you'll cry to God, "Lord, if you choose to do this for me, do it."

Even in this encounter, you may not make the demands. You must say to the Lord, "If *You* choose." In the final analysis, this is all that really counts — Christ choosing what's best. Even then it takes a real man to accept His choice.

Prayer: Lord, until now I really haven't sifted out life's most important things. Too many trifles keep cropping up on my priority list. Give me the wisdom to determine what is most important and then concentrate on that for Your glory. Amen.

26. BOTHERING GOD

Scripture: A man named Jairus, who was a ruler of the synagogue, came and fell at Jesus' feet, imploring him to come to his house, for he had an only daughter about twelve years old, who was dying. . . . While he was yet speaking, a messenger came to the ruler of the synagogue, to say, Thy daughter is dead; do not trouble the Master. Jesus heard it, and said to him openly, Do not be afraid; thou hast only to believe, and she will recover.
— *Luke 8:41, 42, 49-51, Knox*

Many men like to solve their own problems. And while they view their more dependent fellows, they look with disdain upon them. To them, dependence upon someone else is a sign of weakness. To understand that a person might need moral support in a time of crisis seems beyond their comprehension. But when a crisis comes to *their* doorstep, then it's quite a different story. Then they understand the story of Jairus and his dying daughter.

When a crisis comes into the lives of some of these men who have been so independent, often they can't understand why, when their need for help is so great, others pass them by. They fail to realize that their own personal attitude has simply come home to roost. Crisis hours are lonely hours. And the hardhearted man learns this quickly when he is in the crucible.

Notice that Jairus came and "troubled" (or "bothered," as translated in *Good News for Modern Man*) Jesus about his dying daughter. He had faith in this Healer from Galilee. He was sure that Jesus would restore her to full health. He didn't question Christ's credentials as other Jewish leaders tended to do. He expressed simple faith.

Unfortunately, others crowded in the way and hindered Jesus from coming with Jairus immediately. There were many others who made it a habit of turning to others, especially to Jesus, to solve their problems. Many in the crowds probably had tried every home remedy known. Many had probably felt sufficient unto themselves until a crisis hour. Then they were willing to wait in line to even touch the Master's clothing. By the time Jesus was free to follow Jairus to his home, a messenger appeared and said, "Forget it. Don't trouble the Master. Your daughter is dead!"

From all appearances, nothing could be done. Even Jesus was too late to remedy the situation. While she was facing the death hour there was hope, but as soon as she died all hope was gone. Let Jesus go back to helping the living sick. What could be asked of Him now that the girl was dead? So the advice, "Do not trouble the Master," seemed acceptable.

Fortunately, Jesus heard the advice. And being God in human flesh, He didn't feel that this was a matter of being troubled. He took the matter out of their hands and told Jairus not to fear but to have faith. His daughter would recover!

Before bringing the girl back to life, Jesus dismissed the skeptics and the scoffers from the home. Then, in the presence of the wondering parents, He raised the girl from the dead. Surely this result made "bothering" the busy Great Physician in the first place worthwhile.

It really isn't a mark of manliness to "not bother" God. It's a mark of egotism. The man who thinks he can get along without God is self-deceived. He has placed himself on the throne of his life without realizing that the throne is too small and the personalized king exceedingly powerless. To "not bother" God reveals a lack of understanding of the character of God. Such a stance infers that God is not interested in the intimate concerns of the individual. Such a stance intimates that the small king on the throne knows more about himself and his personal future than the Creator and Sustainer of the universe knows about him. To "not bother" God reveals that the person believes that Christ is some far-off deity rather than a personal Lord and Saviour.

The advice of the messenger, "Do not trouble the Master," serves to lead another person into the same false concept of self and God that the one giving the advice possesses. Our Christ *wants* to be bothered. He welcomes the tugs of humans upon His robes.

He invited the people of His day upon earth to come to Him. His invitation still reads, "Come to me, all you that labor and are burdened." He gets great satisfaction out of satisfying the needs of His children.

"Bothering" God? Not from His point of view. And not from the point of view of the now humble person who has come to the disappointing end of depending on his egotistical self.

Even if you have reservations about "bothering" God with your concerns, go ahead and do so. The results will always far exceed those that you're capable of bringing about for yourself. They'll have elements of the miraculous in them. That's the way God works!

Prayer: Lord, I've sung about taking everything to God in prayer, but I haven't really meant it. Help me to overcome the confidence I have in myself. Open to me the glorious vision of what Christ has done and is doing in the world. Then let me allow You to do what You'd really like to do in my life and in the lives of those about whom I'm concerned. Amen.

27. WHAT IS YOUR THANK QUOTIENT?

Scripture: As he was going into a village, ten men that were lepers came toward him; they stood afar off, crying aloud, Jesus, Master, have pity on us. . . . One of them, finding that he was cured, came back, praising God aloud, and threw himself at Jesus' feet with his face to the ground, to thank him; and this was a Samaritan. Jesus answered, Were not all ten made clean? And the other nine, where are they? — *Luke 17:11-18, Knox*

All of us have memories of childhood experiences when we forgot to thank someone for a kind favor or a gift. Our parents made us feel quite embarrassed or ashamed. "Did you say thank you?" they demanded. If we said we forgot, usually they didn't accept our excuses. "It's about time you remember to say thank you to others. The next time you forget, you're going to take it back!" After such scoldings we determined we'd never forget to say those magic words. Then another occasion popped up and we promptly forgot. You guessed it, our parents went through the same shame routine.

Forgetfulness in manners might be excused in a child, but what excuses can adults offer? Why do so many so-called mature humans fail to say thank you at the appropriate time? Why are we so often among the nine rather than being the one? What is our thank quotient?

As we consider the story recorded by Luke, we can point out several good reasons why all the ten should have come back to praise God. First, Jesus paid particular attention to a minority group — even worse, a despised minority group. There wasn't any reason beyond compassionate concern for Him to pause and even look at them. Others despised them; He showed love. Why was He so different?

Secondly, they were cured of life's greatest malady — leprosy. Now they could reenlist in normal society. Now they could have fellowship with the fair-skinned. Now they could get regular employment and would no longer need to depend upon begging. Now they could enjoy the full benefits of their religion. Wasn't that enough to walk even a mile or two to say thank you to the Healer?

Ah! But *one* returned. Didn't he make up for the others in the extensive thanks he offered? He came back "praising God aloud" most likely so others could hear him. He was unashamed of what Jesus had done for him. Next he "threw himself at Jesus' feet with his face to the ground." He worshiped the Healer in giving thanks. He showed his thankfulness as well as shouting it.

Interestingly, Luke adds "and this was a Samaritan" as if to say, "this is the fellow no one would expect to come back." But it's the unlikely one that usually is thankful.

Jesus' question, "And the other nine, where are they?" is significent and soul-searching. They were all cured. They enjoyed the same benefits as No. 10. They probably told *others* that they were cured by Jesus. But why didn't they come back to say thank you?

Here's where we have to do some of our own soul-searching. How thankful are *we* to God? Do we glibly thank Him in general phrases and forget the particulars? Do we simply accept all the God-given good that comes our way without thinking it's something special?

Thanklessness usually evidences a self-centered person. Such a person takes all he can get. He even believes he deserves a lot more than what has come his way. Up to this point he has been cheated. Up to this point he hasn't received all his due. What he gets out of life and from others he feels he deserves. Inwardly he feels, "I had this coming to me."

Before you proclaim that you'd never be so thankless, check your scorecard. When was the last time you really showed appreciation for some good someone did to you? When did you make a special effort to say and show your thanks? When did you last spell out your thankfulness for specific things that God has done in your life? Are you hiding behind an unexpressed thankfulness that reveals a thanklessness? Are you No. 10 or one of the nine?

Maybe it would have hurt the pride of the nine to come back. Maybe it would have inconvenienced them to return. Maybe they would have had difficulty humbling themselves before such a Person. Maybe they were so used to saying a meaningless thank you whenever someone dropped a coin into their tin cups that they would be unable to formulate a meaningful and sincere thank you. Maybe . . . but they were without excuse.

Maybe you have similar problems. Maybe . . . but *you* are without excuse. A genuine Christian is always thankful and makes it a special point to say so by life and lip. Don't let some unconverted Samaritan be "more Christian" than you.

Prayer: Lord, melt my thankless heart so I'll always express appreciation to both God and men. Accept my particular thanks for direction, healing, salvation. May I always be No. 10 on

the thank list — always first to express by word and deed that
I am thankful. In the name of Him who constantly looked up
to heaven and gave thanks. Amen.

28. THANK GOD! I'M NOT LIKE OTHER MEN

Scripture: To some people who were confident that they themselves were upright, but who scorned everybody else, He told
the following story: "Two men went up to the temple to pray, one
a Pharisee, the other a tax-collector. The Pharisee stood and
said this self-centered prayer, O God, I thank you that I am not
like the rest of men, robbers, rogues, adulterers, or even like
this tax-collector. I fast two days in the week. I pay a tithe on
everything I get." — *Luke 18:9-12, Williams*

Familiar parable. Familiar application — humble receive forgiveness, proud do not. Yet there's a lot more in this story, a lot that
is possibly overlooked — a lot that we often bypass in trying to
make the Pharisee out as a real scoundrel.

Today let's look at some of these other aspects. Let's keep the
tax collector in the background and still retain the forgiveness
pitch made at the end. Let's take a good look at the Pharisee. But
be careful; he might be nearly identical to the person you see in
the mirror!

The religious direction of the Pharisee can't be criticized. He
went to the temple to pray. What's wrong with that? He went to the
commonly accepted prayer meeting place. He went to the temple
to indulge in what has been called the most intimate religious
experience a man can have — prayer — conversation with God.
The twentieth-century person who follows this far in the Pharisees's footsteps is going in the right direction. In fact, getting to
church for the purpose of praying would be revolutionary in the
lives of a large percentage of today's Christian men. The Phari-

see's motive outside the temple square was good — he was going inside to pray.

Unfortunately, like many modern men, he blew it when he got inside. He had the right form and probably the correct physical posture (or at least the accepted physical posture), but the content of his prayer was such that Jesus could have descriptively said that, "His prayer bounced off the ceiling." In other words, it just didn't get through. God's ears weren't penetrated by his petition.

The reason for this was simple: He wasn't praying to God. He prayed "the self-centered prayer." How easily he fooled himself. He believed that God was listening. He was absolutely sure he was correct in what he was saying. He was even thankful — something a lot of "give me" believers fail to be.

So far, how does he resemble the person in your mirror? Have you ever fooled yourself in your prayers — directing your words Godward while kneeling with tightly-closed eyes? (The Pharisee probably peeked because he noticed the tax collector nearby.) Have you ever compared yourself to others while in the praying position? You were thankful that you weren't like the rest of men. You were thankful for your religious accomplishments. You were even thankful that you were not like your former self.

Notice to whom the Pharisee compared himself. He took some recognized horrible examples: robbers, rogues, adulterers. For good measure he added one that might possibly have some good characteristics, although the Pharisee probably never recognized them as such. "Lord, I'm not even like this tax collector."

We evangelicals have a tendency to follow this line of reasoning when we pray as well as when we talk to others or contemplate our own characters. We're not like the rest of men. By this we mean that we are *better* than they. Look at the rest of men: murderers, rapists, embezzlers, lawbreakers. We have the tendency to point out the real scoundrels. Surely we're better than they. Surely even the Lord ought to recognize this.

The danger of being proud of our religious position lurks near all of us. It's so easy to compare ourselves with those who are less than we are or to those whose moral standing doesn't meet the accepted norms. It's so easy to boast of the grace we have received, being smug about how God has blessed us and not others. It's so easy to think we are God's favorites simply because we have met our evangelical culture's requirements. It's so easy to believe that others won't receive as great a blessing from God because they're such great sinners or they don't pray the way we do.

Then we read the rest of the parable! "But the tax collector stood at a distance . . . 'O God, have mercy on me, a sinner!' I tell you, this man, and not the other, went back home forgiven and accepted of God. For everyone who exalts himself will be humbled, but whoever humbles himself will be exalted."

Have you ever thought that the tax collector was the one who could rightfully (though he never did) pray, "O God, I thank You that I am not like other men"? He could pray it not out of Pharisaic pride, but out of the distinct position of being set apart by God from other self-centered men. He was different: repentant, humble, and above all — forgiven!

Prayer: Lord, help me to see myself as I really am — a proud, self-centered person as much in need of continual forgiveness as any other man. Give me the manly ability to even beat upon my breast and cry out for pardon. If I ever compare myself to others, give me the courage to pick models that are better than myself. In the name of the humble Christ. Amen.

29. THE WALK BACK TO THE SHIP

Scripture: Jesus came to them, walking on the sea. . . . the disciples were terrified; they said, It is an apparition, and cried out for fear. But all at once Jesus spoke to them; Take courage, he said, it is myself; do not be afraid. And Peter answered him, Lord, if it is thyself, bid me come to thee over the water. He said, Come; and Peter let himself down out of the ship and walked over the water to reach Jesus. Then, seeing how strong the wind was he lost courage and began to sink. . . . And Jesus at once stretched out his hand and caught hold of him. . . . So they went on board the ship. — *Matthew 14:25-31, 32, Knox*

Sometimes the verbalization of a man's faith far exceeds that faith itself. Somehow, no matter how mature we've become as men, we have a tendency toward boasting. We even like to make good impressions on other Christians — as if to admit that if we didn't have a superb faith it would lessen us in the eyes of fellow believers. We've become masters at putting up the big front.

Then suddenly our faith is put on the line. A test comes that completely shatters any sham. We either have it or we don't. That's what Peter found out!

Peter's big mouth led him into a unique experience — the only man known to walk on unfrozen H_2O. "Okay, Lord, if I'm just not seeing things, call me out of this ship to walk on the water." Jesus said nothing about Peter's boastfulness or lack of thinking things through. He simply said, "Come."

But it took only a few moments to see that Peter's faith was shallow. While going toward the Saviour the waves were a challenge to his footsteps, but suddenly he heard the wind blow. Suddenly his faith was exposed to circumstances. Suddenly the real size of his faith became apparent. Suddenly his faith couldn't keep him above water — and he began to sink. The only thing he could do was cry out, "Lord, save me!"

At that moment, before Peter went under — and you know how fast someone sinks into water — Jesus put out His hand and caught a grip on Peter. At the moment of crisis, when a man knows he can do nothing on his own, he'll cry out to God. And God has a way of rewarding such an admission of personal weakness. In Peter's case — Jesus rescued him from the *waves*. In your case it will be a totally different situation. But remember, God doesn't decide to help you on the basis of what He knows about your faith, but upon the basis of His power and planning. Jesus even chided Peter with a question before they got back to the boat: "Why did you hesitate, man of little faith?"

We don't hear much about the walk back to the boat. Why not? Didn't they have to cover the same distance that Peter had walked going out to the water-walking Christ? Didn't the same significant changes in natural phenomenon occur? Why didn't Peter ever describe the feelings he had on the return walk?

First, let's remember that on the walk back to the boat, Peter wasn't boastfully trusting his own faith. He was trusting fully in Christ's power to get him to safety. He wasn't challenging the Lord; he was simply holding on tight. Christ was keeping him up — that's all he wanted.

Secondly, notice that link between Peter and the Lord. It wasn't Peter's power that kept his feet on the water's surface; it was the power of God in Christ. The outstretched hand of the Lord performed the task. The holding power of Christ kept Peter from sinking.

The next time you are tempted to boast of your faith, either in words or in a demonstration, remember Peter. And remember that Christ let him trust his own faith until it proved itself superficial. And when you've exposed your superficiality, remember that Christ is always available. He'll always stretch out His hand and catch the man who realizes that only Christ can save. The walk back to the boat will be a pleasurable experience of trust in a trustworthy Lord.

Prayer: Lord, I fear what my faith would look like if you X-rayed my soul. Give me the courage to look at the film and see how cowardly I am. Then help me to become a real man, a man who doesn't depend upon himself or boast of his faith. Help me to have that same closed-mouth type of faith that Peter had as he walked back to the boat. Amen.

30. ON BEING LONG-NOSED

Scripture: A large crowd of the Jews found out He was there, and they came, not only on account of Jesus but also to see Lazarus, whom He had raised from the dead. But the ruling priests decided to kill Lazarus too, because he was the reason many Jews were going over to Jesus and believing in Him. — *John 12:9-11, Beck*

It almost seems that a fellow can't help himself. An astronaut comes into town; a one-of-its-kind of machine for his trade is being demonstrated a few blocks from his office; a large building is gutted by fire; youth begin to gather for a march to city hall — and a fellow just has to see. So he becomes a spectator.

You can imagine the excitement in the little town of Bethany — where about 99.9 per cent of life was routinely monotonous. Then Jesus came. He always attracted an excited crowd. But on top of this attraction there was an alive dead man. Lazarus had been in the grave for several days. His body probably had begun to decompose. Wouldn't it be a curiosity to see him? Wouldn't any of us desire to talk to him and find out what it really was like to die? Surely he'd have some of the secrets about death and how it felt to enter the hereafter. Surely his testimony could not be refuted. His story would make a front cover feature in any twentieth-century magazine, especially if there were on-the-spot photos. And his first person account would attract a large readership. So what's wrong with being in the "examine Lazarus" crowd? Possibly nothing. Possibly much!

First of all, let it be said that there's nothing wrong in having an inquisitive mind. Curiosity has mothered many good inventions and many constructive changes in society. Those who take the time to investigate have a better chance to contribute something to society than those who hear nothing, see nothing, do nothing. Those who are never satisfied with their present knowledge, and who investigate and research, often become the leaders of our society.

God satisfies the inquiring mind — especially when that mind investigates the eternal truths of the Bible. God reveals Himself more fully to the seeker after truth. The person who gets long-nosed about studying the Bible will find resources previously unknown to him. Paul's admonition to "study to show yourself approved unto God, a workman that needs not to be ashamed" comes to every man. An inquiring mind is a spiritual asset.

But what are the negatives of being long-nosed? Probably the greatest negative is to come simply as a spectator — to be momentarily entertained and then to go away unchanged. Many in the Jewish crowd saw Jesus and Lazarus — and then went away much as they had come, impressed perhaps, but unchanged. It was no different than going to see a sporting event — except that Jesus never made it a habit to entertain people for entertainment's sake. Since He probably spoke to the crowd, He probably challenged them to change their ways of living — to even become His followers. But there's no record that they joined up with Him. Nor is there any record that they were much impressed by the alive dead man's presence. On other occasions when people encountered the amazing Christ, they usually went away telling others about what He had done. This time the crowd is recorded simply as one among several — a previous crowd had challenged Christ's teachings and the next day a crowd welcomed Him openly into Jerusalem.

How easy it is to join the spectators — whether it be at a football stadium, a hockey arena, an automobile show — or an evangelistic rally or church worship service. This can be particularly true when a special speaker is present. A representative of foreign missions comes to tell what God is doing in West Irian. We come to listen to him — but do very little about what he says. A dedicated gospel singer puts on an hour-long sacred concert. We come to view and to listen — and go away saying how beautifully she sang. We are spectators, not participants. Possibly an hour later we'd have difficulty naming more than three of the songs she presented. And the message of the songs probably disappeared almost immediately.

There are subtle dangers in being long-nosed. Unbeknown to the long-nosed person, he begins to take this spectator attitude toward too much in life. As time goes on it takes more situations of a still more spectacular nature to challenge him to make changes. Soon little or nothing challenges him. He could see an alive dead man and then go away and say, "So what!"

Take inventory. Why did you go to your church worship service last Sunday? Why did you listen to that last radio preacher? Why did you attend that last men's brotherhood meeting?

Did you go because you were open to the challenges presented and because you wanted some words that would motivate you to live more like Jesus Christ? Or was it a matter of simply being long-nosed?

Prayer: Lord, I confess that I've often been nosey instead of being an inquirer when attending religious functions. Give me an inquiring mind that will only be satisfied as it absorbs eternal truths and translates these into life-changing experiences. Amen.

31. JOINING THE CROWD

Scripture: Just as He was approaching the city, going down the Mount of Olives, the whole throng of the disciples began to praise God exultantly . . . Blessed is the King who cometh in the name of the Lord; Peace in heaven and praise on high! — *Luke 19:37, 38, Williams*
Then Pilate again appealed to them for he wanted to let Jesus go. But they continued to shout at him, "Crucify Him, crucify Him!" — *Luke 23:20, 21, Williams*

Crowds attract. Get a few friends to stand on a crowded sidewalk. Have them all stare almost straight up at a tall building. Soon others will join the crowd, some not even bothering to find out what the original group was looking at.

Whenever a man walks into a group of men having a good time, he's invited to "join the crowd." Whenever a few high school students want to do something exciting or something slightly prankish, they try to solicit interest from a few crowd joiners.

Usually, unless its a crowd of disgruntled bus or plane customers waiting for a late conveyance, crowds are exciting. We've all joined a crowd at some time or other.

Once two presidential candidates were to speak in the same large city at the same stadium on two consecutive nights. The author and several tract passing friends "joined the crowd" — not to listen to the Democratic candidate on the first evening and the Republican candidate on the second evening, but to distribute Christian literature. Excitement abounded on both occasions. People cheered. The candidates waved, denounced each other's policies, called for massive marches to the polls. As a group of tract passers, we felt doubly rewarded. In the two evenings we handed out nearly thirty thousand "How to Vote" leaflets with a gospel message in each.

In the passages quoted above, Luke tells us of two crowds

which attracted joiners. The crowds were made up of opposites, but not Democrat-Republican opposites. One readily lives with such political "opposites." But the crowds that centered around Christ were life and death opposites. One crowd cried out, "Long live the King." The other jeered, "Crucify Him, crucify Him." One wanted Him placed on a throne; the other demanded He be nailed to a cross. One followed out of devotion; the other charged out of hatred.

Although none of the gospel writers say so, there's a possibility that some of the joiners of the triumphal entry crowd found another opportunity to vent their emotions a few days later near the judge's quarters. It's so easy to get caught up in the crowd spirit that a person really doesn't care what the crowd cheers or jeers about.

Many people in and around Jerusalem hadn't really committed their lives to this Jesus, so they could be spectators in either crowd. Most likely they enjoyed the festivities of the first crowd, but what could they do about changing the second wild gathering? — they weren't in charge! And once a chant gets going, it's so easy to start mouthing the words without thinking about their meanings.

During the past few years, the crowd approach to championing a cause has become popular. An organization's leader announces that a march will be held on a downtown street on a specific day. Organization members come, special signs are made for the event, special chants are composed. Then the big day comes. And you notice that as soon as the affair gets awalking, many *spectators* fall in to swell the marching crowd. Some join the chants — even with a grin on their faces!

By thus joining the crowd, some people unwittingly join people with whom they would disagree in private conversations. Suddenly they find themselves telling the world that they believe something they really never thought through. They're in the *hate everyone* crowd!

A man has to choose his crowds with care — especially if he identifies with Jesus Christ. Some of today's crowds that talk *about* Him aren't really *for* Him. And even some crowds that give loud lipping about being for Him really deny Him in their attitudes toward other marchers.

This doesn't mean that a man shouldn't join up. He should investigate the crowd before he makes a commitment. Then, once that commitment is made, then be manly enough to give it all you've got. Possibly you'll have an opportunity of a lifetime to go into the streets and shout, "Blessed is the King who comes in the name of the Lord."

Prayer: For fear of being identified with the wrong crowd, I have often been too chicken to join any group willing to show its convictions by public demonstrations. Put starch in my spine and energy in my legs for some of the worthy, though possibly unpopular, causes that need my support in this world. Help me to discern between the crowds that do no good and those whose ultimate purpose is helpfulness toward others in which You have great interest. Amen.

32. HAVE YOU EVER BEEN UP A SYCOMORE TREE?

Scripture: Entering Jericho he made his way through the city. There was a man there named Zacchaeus; he was superintendent of taxes and very rich. He was eager to see what Jesus looked like; but, being a little man, he could not see him for the crowd. So he ran on ahead and climbed a sycomore-tree in order to see him, for he was to pass that way. When Jesus came to the place, he looked up and said, "Zacchaeus, be quick and come down; I must come and stay with you today." — *Luke 19:1-5, New English Bible*

How much effort do you put forth to establish an intimate acquaintance with Jesus Christ? Would you go out of your way to have special contact with Him? Would you climb a tree if that would help?

Of course, you don't have to do anything physical to come into contact with the Lord. He's available at your faintest whisper or loudest outcry. He's as near as your breath. By the Holy Spirit's indwelling, He's available in an intimate and immediate way through your thoughts. At least that's what we believe theologically.

But transport yourself back to Zacchaeus and his encounter with the Master. Possibly you're a little shorter than the average so you can empathize with the superintendent of taxes. Even all his riches didn't make him one inch taller. Zacchaeus wanted to see Jesus but just as the opportunity came a group of tall fellows pushed in front of him. This didn't stop the ingenious tax man. He ran ahead of the slow-paced crowd and climbed a sycomore tree. Thus he was immediately taller than the crowd. Christ rewarded the persistence of this little fellow not only by locating him in the tree but by inviting himself to his house for a meal and possibly lodging.

Now getting back to us. How much of the Zacchaeus spirit do we possess? Not that we need to exert strenuous physical effort to make contact with our Saviour, but do we exert that spiritual determination that receives commendation and attention from our Lord?

Let's face it, men — most of us are spiritually too lazy to do much to improve our relationship with our Lord. We read a short chapter from the Bible; we pray limited prayers — often a repeat of what we've said hundreds of times before. But we do little to expand our knowledge of the Eternal One; and we often find excuses why we shouldn't get too involved in the work of His church. Some of us are even physically lazy in these relationships — we fall asleep about half-way through a chapter or two-thirds the way through a rather rote prayer; we conserve our energies for our forty-hour workweek and expend little of it by attending to some church outreach efforts.

Zacchaeus put forth extra effort to gain an effective encounter with Christ. Whether he received scratch marks on his legs from the sycomore bark or whether it hurt the dignity of a rich man, these didn't matter. He wanted to see Jesus and was willing to go up a sycomore tree to accomplish his desires. Christ rewarded his efforts with special attention.

How great must have been his joy when Jesus looked up into the tree and called up to him, "Come down, I want to stay at your house." He got more than he bargained for. Up to that point he probably thought he'd simply fulfill his desire to see what Jesus looked like physically. Now he had the opportunity to see something of the character of the Master. Now he had an opportunity to talk intimately with Christ. Now he had the opportunity to entertain the Lord of heaven and earth!

Is it wise to speculate what would have been the results if Zacchaeus hadn't sprinted ahead of the crowd, ruffled his expensive robes and, undignified-like, climbed a sycomore tree? He would never have had a good glimpse of the Lord. He would never have had any conversation with Him. He would never have been mentioned in the Bible. He would never have had the inner satisfaction in later years of a man who could remember a personal meeting with the Lord Jesus.

What price do you pay when you don't put any effort into improving your relationship to Jesus Christ? Possibly only you and He know. Possibly even you don't know. Possibly you're satisfied with your spiritual status quo. Possibly you'll never climb a sycomore tree (literally or figuratively) to get to know Christ better. But thank God, some men are manly enough to be tree climbers. And they are the ones who see Jesus.

Prayer: Holy Spirit, give me the ambition to pursue a better relationship with Jesus. Let my spirit exert the effort to climb up from where I am to where I ought to be. If climbing a tree will produce results in my inner life, give my legs the energy to push upward. Amen.

33. SLEEP ON NOW

Scripture: He said to them, "My heart is breaking, it almost kills me! You must stay here and keep watching." Then He walked on a few steps . . . and kept praying that if it were possible He might escape the hour of agony. . . . And He went back and found them asleep. . . . He came back the third time and said to them, "Are you still sleeping and resting?" — *Mark 14:34, 35, 37, 41, Williams*

The place: Gethsemane. The situation: Jesus has taken three trusted disciples — Peter, James and John — into the place to pray specifically about the crisis that faced Him in Jerusalem. Right in their presence, verse 33 tells us, "He began to feel completely dazed and to realize His anguish of heart." The burden of the cross seemed too heavy to bear. Could not these three offer comfort and concern during His time of agony? Could they not share His burden?

You know the story. These robust disciples fell asleep. They were more concerned about their physical comfort than they were about Christ's potent struggle. The only evidence of their backbone was a reclining position. In the hour of crisis they chickened out. At the moment they could have been doing the greatest good they were asleep at the switch.

But let's not condemn them too harshly. Rather, let's reinact the scene, bringing it into the 1970s. The place: America. The situation: Jesus has thrust you as one of His chosen followers, not into a secluded garden to pray, but into a secular society to witness. He wants you to be His means of facing the crises of our society. There's the urban crisis. There's the generation gap. There's the drug crisis. There's the militaristic crisis. There's the poverty situation. There's the atheistic thrust. There's the communism crisis. It takes little effort to add to the crisis list.

It's Christ's burden to penetrate all of these crises. He has and is the solution to each one. Nothing is beyond His capacity to solve. He doesn't aim to sidestep any issue. Even though every crisis causes great anguish in His soul either because of the magnitude of the situation or because so few in the situation accept His answers, He does not cringe.

But where are you? Have you joined the Peters, Jameses and Johns who sleep through crisis periods? Have you become wrapped up in your physical comforts or in your own ideas of how to express your faith in comfortable situations? Have you left Christ alone to do battle for Himself?

It's so easy to become self-centered rather than Christ-centered in our living. It's so easy to think of personal comforts and even our well-prepared approaches to life's crisis situations and fail to hear the agonizing of the Lord for those in need.

In many situations the crises pass. There was that needy widow you should have helped a year ago. She's dead now. There was that poverty-stricken family whose house burned down in the middle of December. You could have allowed them to live in one of your empty apartments. But the family has broken up — the children live with poor grandparents; the parents went back to Appalachia. There was that Negro man seeking a home on your street, but you said nothing when other property owners schemed to keep him from buying a for-sale house. How easily the crises of life pass — and we do nothing. We're too comfortable. We need our sleep — be it physical or spiritual.

Paul Rees recently wrote a book titled *Don't Sleep through the Revolution*. The crises within our society have taken on revolutionary proportions. Unfortunately, too many Christians will join the disciples. And the only thing Jesus will have to say to them are the words, "Sleep on now." When the crises are past, volunteers aren't needed.

God sets before you a great privilege as a man. You can be in the vanguard — to face the crises of our world in the name of One who can keep you constantly awake!

Prayer: O wide-awake Christ, forgive me for sleeping during times of crisis. Often my spirit has been willing but my human nature has been weak. I confess it's much simpler and a lot less costly not to get involved. Fill me with more of Your manly spirit — the spirit that compelled You to face and conquer even the crisis of the cross. Amen.

34. BACK TO THE OLD WAYS

Scripture: But there are some, even among you, who do not believe. Jesus knew from the first which were those who did not believe, and which of them was to betray him. . . . After this, many of his disciples went back to their old ways, and walked no more in his company. — *John 6:65, 67, Knox*

There comes a time in every man's life when he has to stand up and be counted. A pressing community issue demands a Yes or No vote. An unpopular decision has to be made at a man's place of employment or business. A family situation demands that a father map out a rather individualistic approach to a problem.

There also comes a time in every man's life when he has to make a decision related to Jesus Christ. You can't sit on the fence all your life. There comes a time when you decide for or against the Lord. You decide either to join up with His Lordship or to follow your own inclinations.

But there also comes a time in the life of the fellow who has "signed on the dotted line"; who has stated his trust in Jesus Christ as personal Saviour; who has joined up with those of like persuasion — there comes a time when this fellow, too, must take a personal stand for the Master.

In such a tight type of situation, the apostle John tells of some men who had followed Jesus up to a point and then turned back to their own ways. They didn't mind being identified among the crowds that listened open-mouthed to the Master's philosophy. They enjoyed the popularity of wearing a Jesus-button.

92

But when He challenged them to share His sufferings as well as His popular moments; when He demanded allegiance as well as affection; when He separated the participants from the spectators; when He tried their faith — "many of His disciples went back to their old ways, and walked no more in His company."

When you're forced to state your identity with Jesus Christ; when the world wants to know the reality of your faith; when Jesus Christ Himself challenges, "Are you for Me or against Me?" — in what direction do you walk? Do you walk toward the Saviour in the confident attitude that asks Him, "To whom shall we go? You have the words of eternal life"? Or do you, like the men John described, "go back to [your] old ways"?

It's so easy to go back to our old ways. The majority of men walk that path. Why buck the traffic just to be going the Jesus-way? Why stand up for Him and be constantly challenged, ridiculed, laughed at by men who make it on their own? Why follow Christ anyway? Can't you make out better in life on your own?

The old ways — some of them highly moral; some of them seemingly even more moral than ways developed by some of Christ's present or past followers — give a constant tug, especially when our faith in Christ doesn't have much starch. The old ways attract especially if a man hasn't really turned from them when he signed on the dotted line at some church or evangelistic meeting. The old ways appeal to the man who tries to have the best (or at least a part of) both worlds — Christ's and this one!

Oddly enough, Jesus did nothing to get them to come back. That's the way Christ operates. He doesn't beg men to keep following Him. He lets them make up their own minds. If they don't want to keep in the straight and narrow, He doesn't force them to stay. At any time in a man's life, he has the full freedom to decide against his former allegiance to Jesus Christ. He can make a decision to go back to his old ways — and either enjoy or endure the consequences. That's up to him!

Thank God there are some like the twelve, who, when Jesus asked, "Would you, too, go away?" answer with a resounding No! Hopefully, you are on this list.

Prayer: Lord, it's so easy to go back to my old ways. Some of those ways weren't so bad; some were enjoyable. But I have decided to follow You. Give me the courage and fortitude to stand in Your corner of life's arena. Let my stand for You help others also to stand. Amen.

35. DOCTRINAL STATEMENTS OR DYNAMIC ENCOUNTERS

Scripture: It was on the same day that two of them were walking to a village called Emmaus . . . discussing all that had happened. They were still conversing and debating together, when Jesus himself drew near, and began to walk beside them; but their eyes were held fast, so that they could not recognize him. And he said to them, What talk is this you exchange between you as you go along, sad-faced? — *Luke 24:13-18, Knox*

Let's retrace the story. Two disciples were going to Emmaus three days after the crucifixion and burial of Jesus. They were discussing all the things that had happened. They were probably confused and disappointed — not being quite able to accept what had happened to their Master. While they were walking along, they debated back and forth. Most likely they thought of the timidity of all of the disciples, themselves included. If only they had had the courage to speak up for Jesus at the trial. If only they had identified themselves as His loyal followers who were convinced that He was the promised Messiah. But now it was too late.

So here comes this stranger asking them why they were debating about current events and why they had become long-faced Christians. Where had He been that He hadn't heard? Cleopas asked Him, "What, art thou the only pilgrim in Jerusalem who has not heard of what has happened there in the last few days?" The news of Jesus' crucifixion had surely gotten to everyone even

94

without modern means of communication. Somehow tell-a-man and tell-a-woman spread the news throughout the city. Yet here was one, apparently, who hadn't gotten the message.

Jesus asked, "What happened?"

At this point the two gave a detailed explanation about Jesus of Nazareth.

Put yourself on that dusty road. Walk in the disciples' shoeprints. What would your thoughts be? How would you react to the stranger if you had no more information than they possessed? Would you take the same intellectual route they took? Would you have been able to recognize the stranger?

Unfortunately too many twentieth-century men are afflicted with the same malady. These disciples were soon cured, however. In contrast, modern men often do not recognize the malady and consequently live with it continually. They possess an accurate doctrinal statement about Christ but never experience a dynamic encounter with Christ Himself.

We're good at explaining what we believe: the Bible is the Word of God; Christ was born of the virgin Mary; Christ died on the cross to take away our sins; He rose from the dead, ascended into heaven, and will return a second time; the church is a divinely instituted body of all those who believe in Christ as Lord and Saviour.

Some of us are proud that our local churches or our denomination requires us and specifically our missionaries, pastors, and denominational personnel to sign a doctrinal statement. Some publishing houses ask their editors to sign a doctrinal statement once a year. Theological seminaries also have this requirement for professors.

But while many are boasting about doctrinal correctness, they show nothing of the love and compassion of the Christ they profess to follow. In fact, they seem to be dominated by narrowmindedness and hate. This is even shown toward others who profess faith in Christ. Many are vitriolic in their treatment of Christians of other persuasions.

How easy it seems to be doctrinally sound and still miss

the dynamic encounter with Christ. Possibly it's the way we've been taught. Possibly we have only become followers of others who specialize in doctrinal soundness but have never personally experienced much of the dynamic encounter with deity. They've systematized everything they believe about Christ. It's orthodox from Alpha to Omega, but it's the "letter of the law" rather than "the spirit." Paul said that the letter kills, but it is the spirit that gives life. Without the dynamic of an encounter with Jesus, what else can you expect but a calculated set of doctrinally correct statements about Him?

When their eyes were opened, these disciples encountered Christ in a living relationship. That put a dynamic into their experience. Suddenly what they believed about Him came alive. They saw beyond carefully worded statements about what had happened in Jerusalem; they saw the alive Christ.

It's true, we need to be doctrinally orthodox, but let's not stop there. Let's not make doctrinal orthodoxy a prerequisite to a dynamic encounter. Perhaps the order should be reversed — a dynamic encounter first, then the doctrinal accuracy. But don't miss out on the dynamic of knowing Christ on a personal, vibrant basis. Don't be an Emmaus disciple that knows all the details, one who could walk and talk with the risen Christ without knowing who He was. Be a disciple that knows Jesus on a friend-to-Friend basis. Dynamic encounters bring a man to the place where doctrinal statements have vitality. That's what this book has been all about. And if you've missed this vitality in your life, you'd better go back and read it over again.

Prayer: Lord, help me to keep the delicate balance necessary between experience and knowledge. Let me see the importance of both and not substitute the one for the other. Let me be constantly sure that my experience contains a divine dynamic that keeps my life alive and vibrant. In Your revitalizing name I pray. Amen.